The sky looks high
John Banner

The sky looks high

John Banner

Silver Fish
publishing

British Library Cataloguing in Publication Data
A record for this book is available from the British Library

ISBN 1 902134 14 1

Printed and bound in Great Britain by
Cox & Wyman, Reading, Berks

Silver Fish Publishing is a division of
Silver Fish Creative Marketing Ltd
37 Pottery Lane, Holland Park
London W11 4LY

Contents

Acknowledgments

My heartfelt thanks must go to my soul-partner Celia, who carried with me the joys as well as the disappointments over a number of years. My family also never ceased in their belief that the vision God gave me by his Holy Spirit was real and authentic. To my children my thanks are due in different ways. For Stephen, who regularly took me aside for prayer and encouragement. For Christopher, whose faith remained firm throughout some of my worst moments. To Nicola, whose level of humour always kept me earthed in reality. To Russell, who constantly assured me of his prayers, and Miles, who just knew that under God 'Dad would do it', and Kerry, who was a constant source of delight and distraction from the regular parish round. I am also grateful to God for giving me Dick Warren, Robert Wickham and John Kain, each an expert in their own particular profession.

For hard work on the computers I must thank Pym Ruperti, Lesley Still and Carol Wharton. Finally I would like to thank my congregation for their wonderful prayer support and encouragement during the difficult days.

Chapter 1

Prophetic beginnings

Our plane circled over Palma airport for half an hour. Celia and I could see the lights of the city of Palma below us. It was October 10th 1964. Our wedding ceremony had just taken place on a very cold and windy day at the lovely church of St. Andrew's in Backwell, a tiny village eight miles west of Bristol. We were blissfully happy with the way the day had gone. After the reception in a colourful marquee in the garden, we set off with my best man, Alan Backhouse, who had protected us from the usual antics of leaving the reception. We made off in his little grey van for the Paradise Motel where our Mini was strategically parked. We had a little time before our flight, and after seeing Celia's friend Jane at Wells Cathedral School we headed back across the moors to the airport. We joined the 'honeymoon special', and after two and a half hours we were on the Spanish island of Majorca.

We were determined to start our marriage by reading the Bible each evening, as this would place God firmly at the centre of our future. What appeared to be a good plan at the time, in fact, proved to be a remarkable piece of prophetic insight. Prior to my call to full-time Christian service, I worked for many years as a gas fitter on a number of major building sites in my home town of Birkenhead. It appeared natural to choose the book of Nehemiah, a man called by God to take charge of rebuilding the walls of Jerusalem. Over the years which were to follow we would often find ourselves finding ruins to rebuild, whether in terms of buildings, situations or people.

I began by sitting up in bed with my Bible open, and started reading, with Celia intent on hanging on every word. Unfortunately

I soon realised that the deep resonant quality of my voice had a somnolent affect upon Celia, and within the space of a dozen verses her breathing developed into gentle snore. A loud cough from me aroused an apology, but within minutes the situation was as before. The result was that our nightly readings were changed to after-dinner readings, and the problem was solved.

Back from our honeymoon I resumed my work as the Curate of St Leonard's in Bootle, and Celia commenced a secretarial job at Russell Engineering Company in the heart of Merseyside's dockland. We stayed in this curacy for three years, during which time our son Stephen was born. The matron refused me entry to the delivery room. This was followed by another three-year curacy in the Lancashire town of Wigan, where Christopher was born at home, and I was there to see him come into the world.

We then spent two years in Australia where I was General Secretary of the Scripture Union of Queensland, during which time our daughter Nicola was born. We returned to the United Kingdom in 1972. That same year I was appointed Vicar of Christ Church, Norris Green, Liverpool, and our fourth child Russell was born. The parish comprised of some twelve to fourteen thousand people situated on a pre-war housing estate. Many problems came in the shape of both people and buildings. Much of the expertise I had picked up on building sites in earlier years was to prove invaluable in this new parish. Together, the men of the church successfully built a new kitchen, toilet blocks with showers, new drains and a number of brick walls in the church complex. These practical times were not without their humourous moments. On one occasion I was under the church floor ripping out the old central heating system, when I heard the distant dulcet tones of Celia calling me. I appeared out of a trapdoor in the floor with the blackest face and hands. With some exasperation and not a little panic, she said: 'You have a funeral darling and the cars are outside.' I leapt out of the hole, replaced the floor cover and ran to the vestry. Within three minutes I was washed, robed and standing at the church door. The cortège following me into the church as I repeated the familiar words: 'I am the resurrection and the life…'

One formidable problem came in the shape of two war-time air-raid shelters behind the church buildings. They were about ten feet high, and built with ten-inch reinforced concrete. They were a constant source of irritation, being a hazard to the young people of the area, many of whom had broken into them over a number of years. Furthermore, they took up a great deal of space. Standing one day in the summer of 1974, looking at this vast amount of brick and concrete, I said: 'I command you to go forthwith!' I promptly went into the house and changed into T-shirt and shorts. I took a fourteen-pound hammer from the workshop, and with a marching whistle I climbed on top of the first shelter and began a demolition job. Over the next three years, with help from Tommy the tramp, a regular visitor who became a family friend, these war-time shelters were completely demolished, releasing a recreation area. During this time Miles Ashley was born. Celia always seemed to have easy and happy births, or at least that's how it appeared from a husband's point of view!

One memorable afternoon, Tommy and I sat on the roof of the shelters and he told me that he had had a bad night previously, and wished to tell me the tale. It was nearly midnight and he had not yet found a place to sleep, and as it was beginning to rain he climbed over the fence of Sefton cemetery and searched for a large grave stone behind which he could shelter from the rain. Unfortunately his nightly sojourn ended up with him falling down a newly dug grave, with the coffin not yet covered adequately. 'That was a heavy landing' he muttered before continuing his story. Having fallen on his face he turned over and to his dismay realised the grave was deeper than his height. The rain increased in intensity. 'Help! Help!' Tommy shouted, but no one came. After an interval of some ten minutes, a distant clock chimed the midnight hour. Meanwhile his cries had been heard by a security guard, who armed with a torch made his way to the unfinished grave. With a giant leap Tommy managed to grip the top of the grave with both hands. The guard, seeing two hands appear from a fresh grave, dropped his torch and ran screaming from the graveyard.

Removing the obstacles of the shelters arrested within me any thought that anything could prevent the progress of the work of God. The deed was prophetic too, for many of the hurdles Celia and I would have to face in years to come would be as significant as the demolition of these old shelters.

Norris Green was a tough area. Celia and I had seen the once-lovely housing estate with its neat gardens and park, complete with rose beds and a bowling green, degenerate over the years into a state of scruffy neglect. After four o'clock in the afternoon the only professional people left in the area were the local Roman Catholic parish priest and me; we had to answer all sorts of problems completely outside our range of knowledge. This may have meant anything from preventing a punch-up in the street to giving refuge to a battered wife and children.

One memorable evening, just before midnight, I went into the study and faced my disorganised desk. Paperwork was strewn all over it. I opened my Bible and began to read, no passage in particular. Perhaps reading the Word of God becomes automatic at times. Anyway, I muttered some prayers for the family and members of the congregation, and reflected upon the day's events.

My thoughts wandered. I looked out through a crack in the curtains to the street outside. A lamp across the road was struggling to illuminate the entrance to the park. In recent months the children had pulled out all the rose bushes, and burned down the pavilion where the man used to sit booking-out the bowls for the green and the golf clubs for the putting. Now the once-lovely area of grass around the roses had been ruined by the feet of amateur footballers. Joe Royal and Steve Coppell both attended Norris Green School.

Gazing across the study, I looked towards the door. Somewhere between myself and the door there stood a figure, a vision. The figure was approximately five feet ten inches tall, with long hair, dressed in white with a darker gown visible from the shoulders. This heavenly visitor gave me a message: 'I want you to build me a new church.' I heard it loud and clear, not audibly but inside my mind. I remained transfixed for many moments, then swallowed, looked down at my Bible, and then looked at the door again. The vision had gone.

My thoughts came back to my Bible study and my prayers. Should I carry on as if nothing has happened? What is this happening? Is it me having a silly picture in my head? Is it a product of a long day in the parish and a tired mind? My pulse was racing. It was now about twenty-past twelve. I struggled with the vision; I couldn't get that picture out of my mind. A presence in my study, a heavenly being, and which church to be built? Where? I quickly examined my thoughts. A church, where have I seen a derelict church? Ah! I know... the church at the top of Bold Street in Liverpool, St Luke's — that's the church to be built.

To give some authenticity to my vision I felt obliged to share what had happened to me with someone else, but who? Who would listen to my ranting at such an hour? I thought: 'I wonder if Maurice is still awake?'

Maurice and Jean Storey, originally from British Guyana, were very firm friends. He was the vicar of St. Luke's, West Derby. We shared a lot together, so I rang him up.

'Maurice, I think I've got a vision. I'd like to share it with you. It might mean a trip into Liverpool at this unearthly hour!' I said.

'Oh... all right... Well, I'll get up. I'll pick you up in a quarter of an hour.'

His soft, chamfered voice bore no irritation despite the late hour. I put down the phone and immediately began to feel idiotic and irresponsible. Yet in some way I was also rather excited. Was God calling me to build this church in the city of Liverpool? Some eighteen months earlier, I had inquired from the Secretary of the Diocese, David Orman, as to the rebuilding of St. Luke's. He said it had been sold to the Liverpool City Council for £90,000 and was now a War Memorial. But to me the derelict church building was a memorial to the belief that God is dead and the church is irrelevant. It was hard and constantly difficult to pass by the church without feeling such an ache and a pain for what it now seemed to represent.

Maurice arrived and after a few greetings we made our way into the city. We parked at the top of Renshaw Street and walked across to the church. It was up a long flight of steps. We walked around the base of the tower, the only piece of the church still left undamaged after the heavy bombardment of Liverpool by the Luftwaffe. Against the backdrop of the street lights, the tower stood out stark and threatening. We stood in silence. Our minds were busy weighing up the permutations. Would we knock down the church and start again? Would we salvage something of the old building, or would it be possible to place within the old shell, a new church structure? Maurice was the first to speak:

'So you believe God is calling you to rebuild it?'

'I don't know Maurice. I just don't know.'

'Well, let's walk around and have a look.'

Picking our way through the darkness we walked around the church. Its walls stood tall and bare, there were holes where the stained glass windows had been. The roof had long since gone, the floor of the nave was now a beautifully kept lawn with seats around the perimeter. Now there were just memories, the passage of a bygone age. We returned to the front of the church and sat on the steps.

'Well, it's a fantastic vision,' said Maurice, 'But what a challenge. What do you think the cost will be?'

I guessed, 'Oh… maybe half a million pounds.'

'Well, if God wants it built he'll provide the money!' said Maurice reassuringly.

A policeman passed by on the other side of the road. I don't think he noticed us. What would he have said? Two clergymen sitting there at one o'clock in the morning! We looked at each other and both grinned.

'Should we call him over?' I asked mischievously.

'We wouldn't be able to explain ourselves.' Maurice replied.

We walked back to the car and sped off up Leecy Street and out towards Old Swan.

'What about a Chinky Lu?' asked Maurice. We soon found a Chinese take-away still serving their saffron rice. Maurice ordered chicken, I ordered curried king prawns, and we went back to the car. Partly choking on a mouthful, I blurted out: 'How am I going to tell this to the Parochial Church Council?'

'Well, that's your problem,' he grinned.

At breakfast Celia and I talked about this remarkable vision. It's true to say that Celia was a little pessimistic. I could almost read her thoughts: 'Here's my husband taking off on one of his hare-brained schemes; leave him alone and he'll come down to earth quite soon.'

The question really revolved around the Church of England's parochial set-up. If God suddenly called me to rebuild St. Luke's in the City, then I would have to vacate the present parsonage. And, if that were the case, then where would we as a family live, for there would be no house with that job. I am sure the Bishop of the Diocese, the Rt. Rev. David Sheppard, would not be interested in the re-ordering of St. Luke's at the expense of a vacancy in my own church in Norris Green. After a meeting on site with my Parochial Church Council, the question in the hearts of the members was 'Where would we find the money?' All I could answer was 'If God wants it then God will provide it.'

Soon an opportunity arose when I could have a talk with the suffragan Bishop of the Diocese. A colleague, Doug Robinson, was being inducted on November 17th 1978 in a neighbouring parish. The Bishop of Warrington, the Rt. Rev. Michael Henshall would be present, and this would give me an opportunity to ask about St. Luke's. At the reception his reply was: 'My dear John, there are more important places to build churches in the diocese than to consider spending money at St. Luke's, which in any case doesn't belong to us.' He switched the conversation, and then, as Bishops do at Inductions, moved on to the next individual. Punctured and deflated, I began to seriously doubt my interpretation of the vision to build a church. Was the Bishop right? If not St. Luke's, then which church and where?

A few nights later I went to the Police Club with my church warden, Norman Farrell. I shared the vision with him. He listened to me sympathetically: 'If the vision is of God, John, then God will work it out!'

My vision, though to me all-consuming, nevertheless did not interrupt the work of the parish. My Reader Tom Cooper and I conducted an evangelistic outreach programme and whole families found faith in Jesus. By October of 1979 I was feeling the pace of the parish and all its demands. I paid a visit to the doctor. I complained of pains everywhere, but before I could get much further with my complaining he suggested that I take myself off on a well-earned break. With no more encouragement required, I promptly informed Celia that I was under doctor's orders to take a rest.

On November 1st I flew out of Manchester airport and headed for Spain and Malaga, then on to Fuengirola. Within the hour of arriving at the hotel, I had strategically placed myself alongside the swimming pool, high up on the roof. I was completely alone and picked a spot facing south. The sun was setting. Within a few minutes a lady came up the lift and surveyed the scene. She was about fifty years old and a little in need of slimming lessons. Of all the places to choose, she conveniently sat down within six feet of me! A few minutes passed. I was struggling not to notice her, when quite suddenly I heard her speak: 'There is still some warmth in that sun isn't there?'

I gave the impression that her presence was a surprise. 'Oh! Yes, there's a little summer left yet' I volunteered.

She turned and faced me. I was flat on my face with my head away from her. The last thing I desired was a lengthy conversation with anyone. I kept on saying to myself: 'You have come here to get away from people, not entertain them.'

'Do you come here often?' she probed. I couldn't believe my ears. That has to be a stock question if ever there was one! I was so tempted to respond in the usual fashion, but knowing the delicate situation I freely admitted that this was my first time.

'What is your occupation?' she continued.

'My job is highly classified' I said, with a little irritation in my voice. She finished her interrogation and, within minutes, moved further around the swimming pool.

This mini-holiday was over all too quickly. I returned to Liverpool and my search for the church that needed to be built.

During 1980 our second daughter Kerry Ann was born much to the delight of Nicola, who now had a baby sister. The year of activity for moving turned out to be 1982. During March Rev. Chris Collins, who had been at St. John's Fairfield, in Liverpool, and was now at St. John's Tunbridge Wells, phoned me one Tuesday afternoon. Chris was aware that I had been unsettled for quite some time. Indeed about a month before he called, Archdeacon Graeme Spiers had encouraged me to think seriously of a move. I had to admit to him that mentally I was only firing on two out of four cylinders. So with Christopher's phone call, there was already a thought that a move was imminent.

'John, there's a parish vacant in the town centre of Tunbridge Wells' Chris began. 'The church is run down, a bit grotty, but I am sure there is a challenge for your style of ministry.'

I had to admit my ignorance and ask Chris where Tunbridge Wells was, for all I knew it was a suburb of London. My immediate reaction to Chris's invitation was partly one of disbelief — surely God wouldn't call me to the South of England! In the eyes of many northern clergy 'going South' was entering the world of afternoon teas, and cucumber sandwiches and, I might add, better expenses.

The thought of joining such a conservative society left me confused that God should call me, if this were the case, to travel South. Chris inquired as to my next day off, and I informed him that it was the following day, to which he replied: 'Then you have a good excuse to come and see this church!' And so I agreed.

I took the 9.05 from Liverpool's Lime Street station. I have always been fascinated with trains and stations, and I gazed at the great dome of this rail terminal. If we were to move south, what would we be leaving behind? As the train trundled through the tight cutting from the station and the bare wet walls echoed the sound of the wheels, I began to think about what I was leaving behind: the River Mersey, so much a part of the folklore of this magical city, the dry Liverpool wit, and the nasal twang of the natives. It was here, amidst the cranes and ships, tall tenement blocks and football fever, that many a comedian was born, from Tommy Handley to Jimmy Tarbuck. Every pub had its comedians. I thought of the swinging sixties, and my management of five boys called 'The Crossbeats'; their guitar music for church consumption was a great hit. As the train moved into the open from the dark canyons of the city I saw an ongoing, almost humourous battle written on the walls of the railway cutting and adjacent buildings. Protestant and Catholic were making their voices heard: 'Long Live The Pope' in gaudy yellow paint had been crossed out and replaced with 'Long Live King Billy'. My thoughts were disturbed by the noise of the tea trolley.

I arrived at Tunbridge Wells and was greeted by Chris. We walked across the main road. Within a matter of minutes we were standing in the High Street. My first view of the church building was not too impressive. A flight of some twenty steps climbed below a triple archway some twenty feet from the level of the pavement. A turreted tower reached up to a height of about sixty feet. Cracks were clearly evident on three sides of the tower. The building was dirty and positively uninviting. Passers by looking at eye level would simply see a flight of steps. For me the building was too massive to fit the small street scene of the neighbouring properties.

On the way back to the station we went to see Holy Trinity, the other church in the town centre. The building was being torn apart ready for use as an Arts Centre. The Church Commissioners had given a twenty-five year lease to an Arts Group, the congregation having left to combine with Christ Church.

We said our goodbyes and I arrived back in Liverpool just before midnight. I kept telling myself, 'It just isn't me. How would my personality fit into a southern middle-class society?' The following morning Celia and I sat at breakfast. I had to confess that I did not warm to the thought of taking on this parish and had freely admitted the same to Chris the previous day. Celia was much more positive: 'It feels right to me,' she said.

Within a week, Rev. David Bubbers was on the phone to me from London. David was the General Secretary of the Church Pastoral Aid Society, and this organisation would make the appointment of a vicar to any one of the parishes under their patronage. So David was a bishop of sorts, for his position was of some influence within the Church of England. 'John, I wonder if you have reached a stage in ministry where you feel the Lord is calling you to pastures new?'

I thought, 'Who has been speaking to whom!'

'I'm certainly open to God's will David. What did you have in mind?' I replied.

'John, I believe there is a parish that would suit you and needs an aggressive personality to take it forward into a new phase of ministry. Would you and Celia consider looking at it and let me know your thoughts and reactions?'

'I certainly will David. Where is it?'

'Tunbridge Wells, in Kent.'

In the days that followed Celia and I became more aware than ever that it was time to move on from Christ Church in Norris Green. This was the second time we were asked to consider a living in the south of England, so a date was fixed to see the parish officially and meet the two churchwardens. 'What will they look like?' we wondered as we stepped off the train. We had been told that Jessie was in her 70s, a retired head teacher, and Roger, a civil servant, close to retirement. We climbed the stairs from the platform and there they were. They had evidently spotted my clerical collar and picked us out from the crowd.

After the initial introductions, we walked across to the church. For me, of course, this was the second visit, but I was not letting on. Outside the church the black stone looked as depressing as ever.

Great neo-Norman arches seemed totally out of character with the smaller shop units in the high street. The steps and entrance below the arches were filthy with pigeon-droppings. The lobby was grey with large flagstones on the floor. A small door led into the nave, which was shaped like a large open box. It had no pillars, and the massive ceiling was suspended from above, bellying a little in the middle. We stood at the back in total silence, each one measuring the scene and awaiting the other's comments. I broke the silence: 'It's big and needing a lot of money to repair it.'

After sitting in the pews I asked a series of provocative questions, 'Do you use the new A.S.B. Service Book? Do you use Psalm Praise? Would you object if we ripped out all the pews and created a central table arrangement? Would you accept dance and drama and other instruments as a part of worship?' To each answer there was a guarded note of acceptance, almost of surrender to the inevitable.

We walked up to the Chancel end where I could see repair work in progress. The builders were outside, and there was scaffolding up to the Chancel roof. 'How much has this cost?' I asked with an air of indifference. 'Twelve thousand pounds' Jessie admitted. I winced physically. All that money spent on a building that was not worth saving.

'On whose authority was the work commissioned?' I prodded.

'The Archdeacon thought it best if the work were done during the interregnum,' admitted Jessie.

Reverend Tony and Gill March were expecting us at the vicarage. It was truly a magnificent building, one of two built by the same contractor. A large oak door presented one with the atmosphere that somewhere there should be a drawbridge. We rang the bell by pulling down a handle to the right of the door. Tony answered. Inside, the hall was oak panelled throughout. A small billiard table was placed at its centre, and French windows looked out onto steps below, leading to the garden.

Tony and Gill were a delightful couple, and I found Gill a very intense person who, after half-an-hour, left me positively exhausted! Tony was just the opposite, quiet, placid and firm. After much small talk, Celia and I, with the wardens, left to see the complex at Holy Trinity. There was no doubt that at its height Holy Trinity was, with its congregation, a force for what was good, right and spiritual. It stood in the very heart of the town. Behind it were two buildings, once the old school, more recently parish rooms, and a caretaker's cottage. After seeing the inside of the church we stepped outside to look at the adjacent property. 'That's the Old School,' said Jessie, pointing to a long single storey building. 'We now use it for meetings.' They were typically Victorian in style, made of local sandstone, approximately thirty yards long. Roger muttered a figure of £200,000 providing there was a will to sell these buildings. My mind immediately shot to the vision I had of a new church, and how much of a hole that would make in the financial outlay. Jessie volunteered to drive us both to see the Crabb Hall, a building across town, once a youth complex, now tenanted by Calvary Free Church. At this point Roger bade us farewell with the comment, 'No doubt we shall be in touch'.

After Crabb Hall we were taken up to St. John's vicarage to have tea with Chris and Vivian Collins, who had preceded us to Tunbridge Wells by about eighteen months. 'Pink gin and Jaguar set or not, we must pray about this call to Tunbridge Wells' I admitted to Chris as he poured out a second cup of tea for me. 'We shall pray as well, that the Lord will make his will plain to you both' he replied. With that we left for the train and home to Liverpool. On the journey we spoke about many aspects of a move. I talked about the usual channels of guidance, the Bible, a senior Christian, facts coming together, and a dream or vision of God's will. It was undeniable that the facts were timely. Our work in Liverpool was reaching a natural conclusion, and people such as Archdeacon Graeme Spiers indicated that 'it was time for a move' to pastures new. Other factors included Chris Collins ringing me up when he did, and Celia's mother saying 'In Tunbridge Wells Celia will be among her own kind!' My two staff workers, Tom Cooper and Mike Millar were doing a good job, and therefore it was easier to leave. The children's education would be coming to a natural break between schools. So, all in all, the parameters for a move were in place. But I still hesitated. 'I want you to build me a new church' kept ringing in my ears.

Two weeks later David Bubbers phoned. David was enquiring about Celia and I visiting the church in question, and our meeting with the wardens. 'We had a most interesting visit David', I said, hedging a little.

'Do you think it's the right appointment for you? It obviously offers a challenge that would suit you John' David interjected.

'I wonder whether it's really me David, it's a far cry from down-town Liverpool. May I have a think about this and get back to you in a couple of weeks?' With that we exchanged pleasantries and hung up.

'I'll be as acceptable as a ham sandwich in a synagogue!' I muttered aloud to myself.

During the evening meal I told Celia, 'That's three times we seem to have been challenged concerning a call to this living. Once from Chris Collins, once from the church wardens and now a third time from David Bubbers'.

'John', Celia prompted, 'you must pray about this call, I am quite satisfied it's right, it's a challenge, it's different than Liverpool, and it's away from your beloved north west of England'.

I knew she was right about leaving Liverpool. What would the rest of the lads think in the diocese, including David my Bishop? John's going soft! He's deserting the cause! He's going where it's easy! How would I face them once they knew? Determined to have a thorough chin-wag with God, I took to the mini-bus and set off into South Lancashire.

Half an hour later darkness was beginning to close in. I passed the edge of Lancashire's new town of Skelmersdale, on through the village of Dalton, and after a further mile or two I pulled over to the left and parked. I felt a little foolish to have come all this way simply to talk with God. The gravity of the situation demanded more than a brief word on my knees by my bedside at home. Gazing through the front window, I noticed a spider had begun to weave a web between the wiper and the glass. He, or she, was acting from instinct. There was no voice of God and no freedom to plan the future, he acted in accordance with a hidden formula known only to him and the Almighty. I thought of the account in the book of Jonah when God ordered a worm to act for him. 'Well Lord,' I pondered, 'I'm more important than that spider or Jonah's worm'.

I cut the engine. There was a deep sense of loneliness as if the mini-bus, purring away over the last few miles, was a measure of comfort and companionship. Outside there was a nip in the air, a freshness, a stimulation. I checked my pocket for my New Testament, and strode off down the road. Green fields turned out to be young carrot tops, row upon row as far as the eye could see. I began to think about all sorts of things other than this meeting with the Lord, the disruption to the family when we moved; the thought of packing up a household so cluttered with years of hoarding items. I strolled a short way and began to talk to the Lord.

'Well Lord,' I said, feeling him very close, 'I've had a calling and I'm not too sure what to do about it. I desperately need an answer. You have asked me to build a new church and I'm more than willing to construct it, but where do you want it built? In Brisbane, Baffin Island, Bolton or Buenos Aires? You name the place and I will give the vision to the folks there.'

Back came the reply loud and clear, 'I've told you three times where to build it.'

I couldn't believe what I was hearing. Tunbridge Wells! Royal Tunbridge Wells! In the heart of comfortable middle-England! I was astounded and shaken. This had to be my shortest prayer time on record. I returned to the mini-bus. I was now ready to tell Celia that our move was confirmed.

It was late when I arrived back at the vicarage. I walked into the study and read a few messages left on my desk. One read: 'Mr Snape attempted suicide again — urgent — call Walton hospital.' After ringing the hospital to check upon his condition, and learning that he was comfortable, I went up to bed. I announced to Celia, 'We are going to Tunbridge Wells! God has confirmed it!'

'I knew all along it was right!' she remarked, and with that we prayed together. The following day I rang the headquarters of CPAS in Fleet Street, London, and spoke personally to David Bubbers.

'David you will be pleased to know that Celia and I believe that God has called us to the parish of Holy Trinity with Christ Church, Tunbridge Wells!'

'Oh! Good, John... Excellent! We shall now set the procedure in motion.'

Within a week or so the church wardens had been informed and also the Bishop of the Diocese of Rochester, Dr. David Say. Subsequently, I was duly informed that my induction was scheduled for mid-November.

I told my PCC at Norris Green, and my two staff workers, Tom

Cooper and Mike Millar. There was much sadness. For Celia and I it was a wrench to leave so many friends who had become very dear to us. We were also leaving my mother on her own in sheltered accommodation. As I was an only child, she would miss my regular visits to her, and the occasions when she saw her grandchildren. Only time would tell how we should solve this problem, with the 200 mile gap.

The work had been tough in Norris Green, but highly rewarding. Now we were in the vicarage clearing out the last bits of our presence with the removal vans outside. To help us with packing we had half a dozen people mopping and cleaning, and generally making the house comfortable for the next incumbent. Before leaving we all stood in the hallway and I prayed a tearful prayer. We stood in a circle and placed our hands on each other's shoulders to say 'goodbye', and left with Miles and Kerry, the two remaining children who were not at boarding school.

My induction on November 15th would formally begin our ministry in the new church. After an evening of rehearsal, I remained in the empty church building. It was a good time to speak to the Lord, and with only the chancel lights on I knelt at the communion rail and prayed. 'Lord, this is a massive undertaking. How am I going to tell this congregation, and its council, that I have come to knock their church down?'

As if in answer, the Lord reminded me that he would give me the right words to say when the time came. I walked over to the lectern, switched its light on and read from Nehemiah 2:11-20.

'I went to Jerusalem, and after staying there three days I set out during the night with a few men. I had not told anyone what my God had put in my heart to do for Jerusalem. There were no mounts with me except the one I was riding on. By night I went out through the Valley Gate towards the Jackal Well and the Dung Gate, examining the walls of Jerusalem, which had been broken down, and its gates, which had been destroyed by fire. Then I moved on towards the Fountain Gate and the King's Pool, but there was not enough room for my mount to get through; so I went up the valley by night, examining the wall. Finally, I turned back and re-entered through the Valley Gate. The officials did not know where I had gone or what I was doing, because as yet I had said nothing to the Jews or the priests or nobles or officials or any others who would be doing the

work. Then I said to them, "You see the trouble we are in, Jerusalem lies in ruins, and its gates have been burned with fire. Come, let us rebuild the walls of Jerusalem, and we will no longer be in disgrace." I also told them about the gracious hand of my God upon me and what the king had said to me. They replied, "Let us start rebuilding." So they began this good work. But when Sanballat the Horonite, Tobiah the Ammonite official and Gesham the Arab heard about it, they mocked and ridiculed us. "What is this you are doing?" they asked. "Are you rebelling against the king?" I answered them by saying, "The God of heaven will give us success. We his servants will start rebuilding, but as for you, you have no share in Jerusalem or any claim or historic right to it."'

Satisfied with this, I made my way home across the dimly lit grove and back to the vicarage.

Induction Day arrived. Bishop David Say pronounced to the congregation that there was 'an invasion from Liverpool!', referring to the number of vicars he had inducted from that city recently. Within a matter of days I was chairing my first Parochial Church Council. In my opening remarks I shared the vision God had given to me.

'I have come to knock your church down and fulfil the vision as God intended,' I informed them. A stony silence followed.

One member ventured a question: 'Surely God intends you to build up his people the church and not necessarily renew the structure?'

My reply was straightforward, 'I believe God will rebuild both congregation and church building.'

The cold dark evenings of winter 1982/83 were upon us. I, like Nehemiah, spent some time coming to grips with the vision I received from the Lord. Nehemiah was assured that the good hand of my God was upon him, and feeling the same faith and confidence, I began to pray concerning the shape, size and complexity of the building. In order to help my vision, I walked the town at night. I could then, with freedom, stop and stare at buildings, pacing without people stopping and looking at me. I walked the Pantiles, a Victorian scene with magnificent old buildings just south of the town; I began to get the flavour of Royal Tunbridge Wells!

At the top of Mt. Ephraim Road there was a set of steps leading up to a suite of offices. In my imagination I could clearly see the same rising up to the entrance of the new church. Back in the High Street I paced out the ruins, for it was quite clear from recent reports that the building required many thousand of pounds worth of repairs. As early as this I could see the church as a derelict mess ready to be demolished. The building was thirty paces wide and sixty paces long. The width was equivalent to five shops on the other side of the street. These measurements included the church hall, which was immediately adjacent to the church. The building was initially erected as a Victorian Theatre, there being no foundation stone laid for a church. However, the builder, convicted of malpractice in the construction of the building, was brought before the courts and summarily sentenced to penal servitude in Tasmania. William Franklin, a local vicar, purchased the unfinished building, and it was consecrated in 1835. But by now the shoddy workmanship was telling, and costing the congregation a great deal of money.

A short while later the full vision came to me of exactly what the new church and hall complex would look like. The very next Parochial Church Committee Meeting, I told the members exactly what was on my mind.

Chapter 2
Holy Trinity and Gahini

Within days of my induction I was taking the midweek Holy Communion service in the old school buildings behind Holy Trinity. These were still being used for the occasional midday prayer meeting for business people and by a scout troop. After the service I quizzed the eight elderly ladies present concerning the continuation of having worship in such a cold and dirty place. Eyebrows were raised, looks passed between friends, and feet shuffled nervously. I remained silent to allow the full impact of what I was saying to sink in.

'Vicar, we do switch on the heaters in the winter as you can appreciate, and this is the last real connection we have with Holy Trinity.'

I will never understand the affection a person can have with bricks and mortar. My ten-year-old Nicola, upon leaving the vicarage in Liverpool, had promptly gone around the building kissing every wall. But it was quite clear after further remarks in favour of staying in this old building, that the ladies had no desire to worship elsewhere.

In these early days I decided to do some parish visiting, and it was at this time that I got to know about the Rwanda Mission. To those of us at Holy Trinity, Gahini is a hospital, but to those in CMS Rwanda Mission, it is more than a hospital. It is a community of Christians occupying a hill in this central African country. Its neighbours are Tanzania to the east and Congo to the west. Gahini is a moderately sized African village, and some short distance away is the small but significant hospital of the same name.

To understand the connection with the missionary society, I need first to explain a few things. Not long after my arrival in Tunbridge Wells I noticed that the church supported no fewer than eleven missionary enterprises. This was not good, I thought, to concentrate the mind of the congregation on so many different directions at once. It was agreed by the church council to reduce these to five, one of which would be Rwanda Mission. I foolishly suggested at one stage that we abandon Rwanda, but there was a large outcry in favour of keeping it on the stewardship books. I was informed that Miss Ferguson would ignore such a decision and carry on regardless. There was nothing for it, and a date was fixed to visit this lady.

The house was situated in a long wide road in the better suburbs of Tunbridge Wells quite near to the Nevill cricket ground. I was looking for a detached house with lace curtains and ivy growing outside, but the house was semi-detached, lying behind a small garden and a winding pathway leading to a porched green door. I rang the bell. The door was opened by the sweetest little lady, all of five feet one inch tall.

'Oh, you must be our new vicar. I am so pleased to meet you, do come in.'

I entered the hall. It was dark and I hesitated for a moment so that my eyes could adjust. To my left flickered a gas fire. On the floor to my right, next to the staircase was a stuffed alligator, six feet long and poised to bite any unsuspecting intruder. As my eyes became accustomed to the dimly lit interior, I could see that almost everything was painted dark brown: doors, skirting board, and a long open staircase running parallel to the narrow hall.

We made our way into the living room. Seated there was Miss Ferguson's companion, Miss Lillian le Page. She was about two inches shorter than Fergie (which I was later to discover was her nickname). She greeted me with such an angelic smile: 'I am ever so pleased to meet you, I've heard so much about you already.'

I thought, was that good or bad gossip? 'Sit down Vicar.' said Fergie. I was given the best chair, and for a moment while tea was prepared, I was given a chance to observe my surroundings. The room was filled with furniture, the walls festooned with all sorts of pictures, calendars, clocks. House plants were in evidence on top of, underneath, behind, growing in and out of pots, vases, and all sorts of earthenware. Outside was a small garden, which in comparison to the numerous plants inside seemed quite bare.

'Can't do much outside this weather, Vicar,' said Fergie, with a certain reservation to her remark.

'Don't worry Kathleen,' said Lillian following her companion. 'It's summer in here today, and we have a special visitor.'

I couldn't help but chuckle under my breath. I'm glad I didn't persuade anyone to abandon Rwanda!

In the hour that followed I learned a lot about the Rwanda Mission. It began largely as a spur from the Church Missionary Society. Apparently two young doctors were addressing the congregation at Holy Trinity Church Tunbridge Wells one Sunday night in 1921, when an army officer, forced to abandon his car for an overnight repair, attended the church service to give thanks for his deliverance during the Great War. On hearing the plea from these two doctors that a country called Rwanda was without missionaries, he wrote a cheque for £500 to get the work started. To Fergie and Lillian, the work began in such a miraculous way that God's Holy Spirit was involved from the beginning, and therefore the work and support of the Mission should not lapse.

From the hallway a clock chimed four o'clock, and glancing at my watch I saw that it was time to move on. Fergie suggested that before leaving the house I should observe the level of their support by visiting the parlour. All over the floor were bundles of sacking approximately fourteen inches square. On each one was a hand sewn label bearing their destination. One bundle had not been completed so I was able to view the contents. There were bed sheets, clothing, coloured blankets made from knitted squares, and a large jar of Marmite.

'They especially enjoy the Marmite' said Fergie, with a slight degree of superior knowledge. Why Marmite? I thought. Why not jam or cheese? I bowed to her experience in these matters, she obviously knew what she was doing.

'We tried sending posh boxes, but they were always being broken into… People assuming that there were valuables inside. Sending the parcels this way in sacking doesn't look too expensive,' she informed me.

I put my arm around Lillian's shoulder and said, 'On behalf of Rwanda Mission and our church I want to say a big Thank You for all that you and your ladies are doing for the work at Gahini.'

I got into my car and sat for a little while thinking about these two ladies and their companions working hard to support this small Mission hospital at the very heart of Africa. I was very impressed, and loudly thanked God for them both. Back home I said to Celia, 'I have been to see the Rwanda supporters, and I am now more convinced than ever that we should not only keep Rwanda as a Mission supported by the church, but that we actively increase our giving!'

Many weeks passed. The temperature decidedly took a tumble. It was then I suggested we move the mid-week Holy Communion from Holy Trinity school to Christian Alliance House, some two hundred yards away. This move was acceptable and the last ties with Holy Trinity were severed. Now I could concentrate on selling the old school buildings and begin the process of realising much of the capital tied up in these unwanted properties.

Robert Wickham was first mentioned at a church meeting as someone who may be able to help in handling the sale of the old school halls. For many days I kept noticing the name in numerous places. Was God trying to tell me something? I noticed the name on the rear of a removal van, then at a baker's shop, then at a solicitor's office. I imagined he would be a 'Pickwickian' gentleman of portly stature, a confirmed bachelor, a lover of Georgian antiques, and familiar with all things to do with Beethoven. It was now vitally necessary that I approach this formidable figure and seek his advice and expertise as swiftly as possible. So I rang him and shared the vision God had given to me. He told me of his work for the church at diocesan level as an advisor to the diocesan Board of Finance regarding Glebe investments and he would be happy to offer his expertise if I required it.

It was becoming more clear by the day that the desire of the PCC and congregation to demolish and rebuild the church would antagonise those of the historical lobby. In the Royal Borough of Tunbridge Wells the Civic Society and the Victorian Society were vociferous in retaining the status quo. Some monumental blunders had already scarred the town, not least a development at the far end of the Pantiles and a large car-park right in the heart of the town centre. On December 8th I decided that it was high time I identified the opposition. The Planning Application for demolition and rebuilding would concentrate the minds of the Borough Council, so it seemed right to be aware of who the key personalities were. Three names kept appearing either in conversation or in the local press: Roderick Symon, a retired senior naval officer and chairman of the planning committee; Myrtle Streeton, a member of the Civic Society; and Barbara Sandford. Fully expecting this society to give me a lot of opposition, I took note of each member; particularly those who served on the Town Council.

The following day, I went with Rev. Norman Hutchings, a retired clergyman and a close friend, to St Paul's in Robert Adam Street, London, and spoke with the vicar Rev. George Cassidy. This was a modern church, and there was a lot that we could learn. George gave us a conducted tour, being fair to point out the good things concerning the building as well as the pitfalls. I noticed photographs of previous vicars lined down the walls of the stairs. Two things impressed me: the thought given to generous office space for the church and the commercial income from the car park and a building complex, which also contained the vicarage. Two things left me cold: the regimented pews giving no flexibility for uses other than worship, and the fact that the church had been built by a developer, who on taking the original site of the church in Baker Street had built it down a back street and hence off the main thoroughfare. I had received a boost to the dream of building a new church of which God would be proud.

Two days later I read my Spurgeon's Morning Reading: *'Faithful is he that called you, who also will do it.'* I had my tail up. Christmas came with all its festivities and jollifications. We had a joint party with the Methodist church on January 15th 1983, and all was sweetness and light. However, storm clouds were gathering in our clear blue sky.

Peter Blackwell was a member of the Parochial Church Council and lived fifty yards from the vicarage. He was a transport manager for British Telecom. He was easy to talk to and so I shared with him the vision of a new church on the site in Tunbridge Wells High street.

'There's plenty of money invested in buildings in Tunbridge Wells that the church should realise as the basis for future investment in new property,' Peter proffered. 'I've already looked at the buildings at the rear of Holy Trinity, and I think that's where we make the start and put them up for sale. You could get a quarter of a million pounds for those buildings!'

Encouraged by these statements I went back to Holy Trinity Halls within a few days. Armed with the keys I looked around the buildings. In my imagination I could hear the laughter of children, the voices of the teachers, and almost smell the aroma of wet clothing in the cloakroom. I could hear happy young voices singing 'All Things Bright and Beautiful', and the ubiquitous school bell as the day came to its end. Now it was dusty and the air smelt acrid. I walked across the main hall, locked the two doors and made my way to what was now a Caretaker's cottage, formerly the home of the Headmaster. Mr. and Mrs. Davies, an elderly couple who were well beyond retirement, were the occupants of this delightfully old cottage. This building too would have to be sold with the rest of the property. After a brief word concerning their future, I left.

Anxious now to get an impression of what the new church should look like, I approached Peter Vincent. Peter worked in finance in the City and was a keen historian of the Second World War, especially of the Royal Air Force, and spent much of his hobby time painting aeroplanes and making models for display purposes. Peter was willing to put my ideas on paper. I was delighted to receive the first artist's impression of the finished building just as I envisaged it. Armed with this picture I shared it with my family and friends, and more particularly the PCC. The latter required some convincing but even at this early stage it was quite clear that four or five members out of sixteen could see a real possibility to end the nightmare of spending so many thousands of pounds on repairing the old structure.

I began to reflect in my quieter moments how easily demolition and rebuilding would be acceptable to the various historical societies, such as The Victorian Society, The Georgian Society, Kent Historical Churches Commission, and perhaps the biggest lobby of all, The Civic Society of Tunbridge Wells. It was time to go to the Planning Office of the Town Hall and speak to one or two influential officials, not least the Town Planner and his assistant. So, early in the year I spoke with Gerald Plastow and Bill Hall. I was given an overview of Tunbridge Wells, and in particular a brochure setting out the council's ideas and plans for the next five years. I came back to the vicarage with the policy document in hand and turned to references to do with the church in the Section CP17, and I read the following:

> There will be a presumption against the demolition of churches and ecclesiastical buildings, and against proposals which would irreparably damage their character, or the contribution these make to the town scape, unless an over-riding case has been made, and alternative uses have been proven not to be feasible.

As I read this in my study, I fell back in my chair and felt a sinking feeling in the pit of my stomach. Was I going to be frustrated at the very first hurdle? Would I be allowed to demolish this building? Only time would tell.

March 11th was a sunny day and Dilys, my secretary, was very conscious of the fact that I wasn't in the mood to do too much work in the study. There had been a series of late nights in the previous week, but today was to be a watershed in the life of Holy Trinity with Christ Church. The Bishop of Tonbridge, David Bartleet, was as disappointed as the rest of us that the Western Area Plans Sub-Committee had turned down our scheme. He advised me to lay the whole thing before the PCC and if necessary the congregation, in the form of a covenant, and so get everyone's wholehearted support to build the new church. A lunch meeting with George Duncan, one of England's finest preachers encouraged me to pursue this line of action. I took it therefore that God was in this decision and I should proceed with a document to place before the Church Council. Dilys and I composed the following:

> We, the undersigned members of the Parochial Church Council of Holy Trinity with Christ Church Tunbridge Wells do pledge before God this day our wholehearted commitment to the building of a new church on the site of Christ Church, Tunbridge Wells, to the honour and glory of his name. Dated this 11th day of March, 1985.

We made sufficient spaces for each member of the Council to sign, and at the bottom the following text, taken from Nehemiah 2:17–18.

> *'Let us rebuild the wall of Jerusalem and rid ourselves of this disgrace!' Then I told them about the desire God had put into my heart, and of my conversation with the king, and the plan to which he had agreed. They replied at once, "Good! Let's rebuild the wall!" And so the work began.'*

The PCC had debated the situation, one or two folk had some fears. One person could not see a way forward because we did not possess all the money and therefore could not understand us going ahead with building, knowing full well that the money was not forthcoming. Another remained silent throughout. Yet another made overtures that the financial burden would be too much for us to bear. However, the rest of the Council seemed more positive, particularly after I gave a sermonette on the exercise of faith and reminded those present that 'Without faith it is impossible to please God' (Hebrews 11:6). I simply made the point that so much faith was exercised by the children of Israel in the Old Testament and Jesus desired that we show great faith in the New Testament. In my own experience I had been used of God many times in the face of many impossibilities. This building was no different. I ended by saying that the waters of the Jordan river only parted when the priests were prepared to demonstrate their faith and step into the swollen river. Ten people signed out of a total of fifteen, and while we were not unanimous it was a clear mandate to pursue the vision God had given me. I ended the evening by saying that I believed God had a vision for Holy Trinity to use it again for the church as a radio and television communication centre. A few eyebrows were raised and a few looks passed. Perhaps they were thinking, 'Here he goes again on another hare-brained scheme.'

It was late when I got home, and the family had already gone to bed. I made a cup of tea and turned on the television. It was a political question and answer programme. I thought the interior of the studio looked familiar but to my surprise when the titles came up the caption read: 'The programme tonight came from Holy Trinity Arts Centre, Tunbridge Wells.'

Duncan Bullock came to me one day and greatly encouraged me at a time when the formidable task of what was ahead of us was beginning to loom large and foreboding. How I thanked God for these young, enthusiastic Christians. Duncan had come to the church at the age of fifteen; his parents having split up. Our church took him in and encouraged him to give his life to Jesus, and as a result of his commitment to the Lord he played an active part in the church youth club.

'John, I've got a great idea for fund-raising. Peter Blackwell and I would like to organise an Antiques Auction. The vibrations from a number of the congregational members would suggest that we could make a couple of thousand pounds. Peter and I will organise it, if you so wish?'

I was thrilled with this tangible support from a young man in the congregation and from Peter, who believed that the vision was of God. So the two of them put their heads together and planned the event. The night before the auction, the church was filled with all sorts of antiques, pictures, paintings, vases, cupboards, furniture, and silver. Duncan proudly produced for me a catalogue, complete with lot numbers and brief comments on each item. The services of Cyril Wood, a retired auctioneer, were obtained, and it was quite a scene as the parish hall filled with people the following night with Cyril in true professional fashion bouncing the bids off the walls. The total sum at the end of the day was over £2,500. The new Church Fund had begun!

I was now anxious to realise as much of the capital as I could from the various properties that Holy Trinity had held over the years. One of these properties was Crabb Hall. This building, situated in the heart of the town centre, was a small part of the once extensive building plant belonging to Holy Trinity. Within the Camden Road area, the church had had at one time a number of school buildings. Many of these were sold off to the National Provident Institute, a very large pension concern with headquarters in the town. Of all the buildings that Holy Trinity had owned only two were left, Crabb Hall and a shop at 40a Camden Road. This latter property was once part of the second headmaster's house, now leased by the Brighton Co-operative Society. The present tenants of Crabb Hall were members of Calvary Free Church. Derek Martin, was the Senior Elder. I suggested I meet him and the other elders to place a proposition before them.

Derek was a local magistrate and a well-respected member of the community. He was a businessman and a leading Christian in the town. Our theological persuasions were entirely commensurate to the evangelical cause, and many were the things in the town that often found us on the same panel or committee together. By 8:15 pm I had placed before the elders the possibility of purchasing the freehold of their building for the sum of £25,000. A lengthy discussion followed and it became apparent to me that there was no desire to purchase the freehold as they had recently, in the last four years, re-negotiated a 25 year lease with us. So, a subsequent letter came from Derek confirming the desire to keep things the way they were at present. That evening I wrote in my diary: 'I am convinced that God is going to do a work in both our churches which is beyond our immediate vision.'

Our church prayer meetings were always well attended. Often the vicarage's main lounge would squash some twenty-five people in for this fellowship. For some time I had been exercising the minds of the fellowship to pray effectively for God's guidance regarding the appointment of an architect. Within a matter of weeks the PCC had appointed a Church Development Committee to discuss certain issues such as the disposal of Holy Trinity Halls, the future of the Crabb Hall (Calvary Free Church) and the disposal of the Davies' cottage. We invited Robert Wickham to the meeting. He was in his early forties, slim, thinning on top, always immaculately dressed, and passionate in what he was doing for the Lord. Not a bit like my original vision of him. He advised us to dispose of the Holy Trinity School site and the Davies' cottage, and further advised that we shelve the disposal of Crabb Hall until the time was right, as Calvary Free Church were not interested in purchasing the freehold of their rented property. As I accompanied Robert to his car I asked him whether he knew an architect who could capture the vision of our new church. Without any further thought his reply came, 'Brenda Davison of Hampstead.' I turned and wished him goodnight.

Returning to the house I told Celia, 'We have our architect!' Subsequently Robert made an appointment and Brenda came to the vicarage one afternoon. She was in her early fifties, her greying hair tied with a ribbon in a pony-tail, wearing a long blue dress and chiffon scarf, and carrying a brief case. We sat in the living room and I outlined roughly what the building should look like, and armed with Peter Vincent's pencil sketch, I shared my dreams and God's vision for a complex which would meet the needs of both the church community and the social requirements within the town centre. Brenda listened attentively and, apart from brief clarification, seemed to take it all on board. Within the hour I was saying goodbye and she promising to send some outline sketches. After she had left I went into the living room, sat down and gazed hard at Peter's drawing. I had seen in my minds eye a building fronted by a shopping precinct with a central entrance and a flight of steps entering in to the worship area. Above the church floor were offices and hall complete with fire-escape to the right and an entrance to an underground car park. On the advice of Robert Wickham we had put the Holy Trinity Church Hall and cottage up for sale. The highest figure (£237,000) came from a developer. This was duly accepted by the PCC and invested with the Church Commissioners through the Diocesan Board of Finance.

Chapter 3

A major set-back

In June 1983 we were contacted by a buildings development concern from Birmingham. Bryants were interested in placing an Option to Purchase Crabb Hall, named by a Miss Crabb, who had financed the building in memory of her brother. A date was fixed in mid-July to meet and discuss the details. Altogether we numbered five; developers agent Guy Shearer, Mr. Gillard from Bryants, Robert Wickham, Jack Purvis the church treasurer, and myself. We met in the kitchen of Crabb Hall, a most unlikely setting for a business meeting, but there was a long table and enough chairs so we got down to business. I was under the impression that the meeting could take approximately fifteen minutes, but an hour and a half later we were still there. I had asked a number of people in the congregation to pray for us from 11 am onwards and just before entering the hall we had prayed in Robert's prized vintage Alvis car.

The discussion wandered about all over the place and I frankly wondered whether we would ever talk about money. Finally, the first signs of it arrived in the discussion with, Method of Payment, Duration of Option and Penalty Clauses, this latter item in case the option was not taken up. Guy Shearer then said in a matter of fact way, 'After much consideration, we have considered the price to be £100,000 but to secure the property we are prepared to offer £140,000.'

Robert shot a glance at me, we were seated directly opposite each other, quite suddenly I was aware that all faces were looking at me. Robert lifted his eyebrows, looked down at his papers but didn't say a thing. I quickly did some calculations:

	£900,000	(Possible price of new building)
minus	£234,000	(Sale of Holy Trinity School Hall)
minus	£300,000	(Congregation Contribution)
	£366,000	Balance required

'I would like £375,000 to meet the cost of my new church', I said, somewhat detached from the proceedings. Some twenty seconds of silence ensued in which it was quite clear that all the brains were taking into consideration the figure I had tabled. Guy Shearer replied breaking the silence.

'Reverend, we cannot fix the price of this building according to what you want to do elsewhere in the town. There is a specific cost to this building as it stands.'

The two men then whispered something and Guy Shearer asked that they discuss things in private, and both left the room.

'Robert', I said a little nervously, 'have we overshot our bolt?' 'No, I don't think so', he replied, 'let's wait and see the outcome'.

After ten minutes the two men stepped into the room, stopped in their tracks, and Shearer said, 'Against my professional advice, it has been agreed we offer you £300,000 and not a penny more'.

I looked at Robert and gave the tiniest nod which was hardly discernible. Robert spoke: 'My client and I are prepared to settle at that price'.

We all stood up, shook hands and said our goodbyes. Outside my heart was singing and rejoicing, I wanted to shout 'Hallelujah' on that hot July afternoon.

Within eighteen months the news broke in the local press, on October 12th 1984: 'Shops Centre Plan — Council promotes big mixed development'. Within the newspaper article there was a small but significant reference to 'compulsory purchase powers'. This meant that the town council was to acquire all the land for its development and could offer a price considered by the District Valuation Officer as fair and that price would be the only and final offer. Bryants had been buying up properties and gaining options to purchase in the hope that the development would be awarded to them.

The scheme went ahead as planned and the £100 million project was initially brought together in paper form by Hillyer Parker, who acted for the council in laying out the brief for what turned out to be four finalists for the project: Metropolitan Estates Property Company (MEPC), Speyhawk, Bryants of Birmingham and Norwich Union.

During this period I had taken an Evening Service and was saying Goodnight on the steps of the church. Earlier I had spotted a gentleman in the congregation, in his sixties, about six feet tall, well groomed, thinning on top, with a ruddy complexion. I approached him.

'It's lovely to have you worshipping with us', I said, stretching out my hand.

'Nice to be here, I've just moved into the area. I gather this is my parish church?'

'Where do you live?'

'I have a house in Calverley Park.'

This park, in the heart of the town has many very large stone dwellings, all built in the period when Decimus Burton as an architect, was planning this particular development. Each house was considered to be a substantial investment. We questioned each other for a number of minutes. He wanted to know how long I had been vicar, and I was interested to know his occupation. I discovered that John Kain was a partner with a company involved in building and development. I briefly shared with him the vision God had given me. He reassured me that if I required any help, he would offer his knowledge and experience. So thrilled was I to meet such a man that I forgot to ask him the number of his address. At home I shared with Celia how God was surrounding me with the right people.

Some six months previously the Lord had brought to the congregation a bank manager and his wife, Dick and Joyce Warren. Dick had been a Reader at St Margaret's church in Tenterden some twenty miles away and after moving house, decided after a brief sojourn around the churches to stay at Christ Church. I now had two experts, the one knowledgeable in building, the other in finance. With Robert Wickham an expert in Planning Development and Compensation, the team was complete. It was not long before the PCC appointed John Kain as Project Manager and Dick as the Fund Treasurer. Robert was already our advisor by virtue of having a Diocesan appointment as Planning Consultant.

One quiet afternoon in the parish I visited the Town Hall and asked to see the Hillyer Parker documents. All the owners of the

properties had been methodically listed and Calvary Free Church
(Crabb Hall) was written down in the ownership of Derek Martin.
Hillyer Parker had not done their homework meticulously, for Crabb
Hall belonged to the Church of England and in particular, the parish
of Holy Trinity with Christ Church Tunbridge Wells. On February
12th 1986 the new Chief Executive in the Town Hall was Rodney
Stone. He wrote to me requesting a meeting of all the parties
concerned with the new Victoria Project. MEPC had got the contract
and now issues involving compensation for our lessees and for
ourselves had to be solved; the meeting was fixed for March 7th.

The day arrived, cold and windy, as John Kain, Robert Wickham
and I made our way to the Town Hall. I had left the vicarage full of
people praying for us while the meeting progressed. We met in the
large council chamber. It's size was intimidating as we gathered
around a long polished table. Around the walls were impressive
paintings of regally clad earlier Mayors of the Royal Borough, Scrolls
of Honour with dates and names told the occasional visitor or Council
Member, who were the dignified people that had served in bygone
years. The Coat of Arms 'Do Well and Doubt Not' hung over the
Council Chairman's chair. This I found most encouraging as we
embarked upon these negotiations to fulfil God's vision.

Seated opposite to me was Derek Martin, his new pastor David
Adkins and one other elder. To our left were two reps from MEPC
and one from Hillyer Parker. In the middle, taking the chair, was
Rodney Stone. At the opening of the discussion that followed each of
us presented our case. For Calvary Free Church, Derek Martin
simply stated that they were lease holders in the situation and
wanted to safeguard their social, spiritual and geographical position
within that part of town. Mr. Martin went on to say that he had had
re-assurances from the planning office that the successful developer
would be obliged to build a new church. Now that MEPC was the
developer, he hoped that they would still be under an obligation.

For our part Robert was in good form, and in presenting our case
he made it quite clear a measure of compensation would have to be
in the offing. After all Christ Church were losing a large building
which in terms of the new plans took up a substantial amount of
space. John Kain went further, saying that our building was 'the heart
and lungs' of the new development. Earlier in the town hall I had

seen a model of the proposed scheme and a former mayor had placed a price on our building of £1,000,000. Rodney Stone was quite clear about there being a replacement church for Calvary, but saw that as compensation for us as well. 'After all,' he said, 'You can't have your cake and eat it'. The point at which the meeting broke up was the remark by Mr. Stone that he would contact the District Valuation Officer, Mr. Flann and get a true valuation of the building.

In June 1984 the PCC finally decided by 19 votes in favour and two abstentions, to pass a resolution declaring the church redundant and seeking to submit plans for a new scheme to the Planning Authority. Within days Celia and I were attending a Deanery supper when Canon Mantell informed me that a member of his congregation, Councillor Jim Perry, had proposed a resolution to a Planning Sub-committee that Christ Church building be 'listed' by the Department of the Environment. This move would make our job all the more difficult. It was like water being poured on the sacrifice as pictured in the story of Elijah on Mount Carmel (1 Kings 18:20), and could only bring glory to God. Such a move had been prompted by a visit by the Historic Buildings and Ancient Monuments Commission and also from the Victorian Society.

I went to see Jim Perry, informing him that plans for the redevelopment of the site were well under way. The following day Jessie Rhind, Stuart Wood and I attended a Planning Meeting, and Councillor Perry sought to overturn his previous decision in having the building Listed. At a Town Hall meeting of the borough councillors, the committee voted by 29 votes to 9 to defer the matter.

Arriving home that evening, I discovered that Celia had left a note by the telephone for me to contact my mother's social worker, Sue Berry. She had informed us that my mother was fretting for us as a family. We had been away for three years, and I couldn't make the journey to Merseyside too often. Celia and I decided to bring her down to Tunbridge Wells, and we found a nursing home in Rusthall. I loved my mum, and to think that she had given me birth with such trauma, and had received a promise that the fruit of her womb would be blessed, filled me with great awe. Many were the occasions when I would wonder how much longer she would be with us. Her speech was becoming slurred, her movements slower. I would leave her room with a kiss on the cheek, lovingly shut her door and within moments, stand outside below her window waiting for her to appear. She would wave and give a happy smile. Despite the fact that she had lost a leg some thirty years earlier, she always possessed a vivid and deep sense of humour.

February 26, 1985 was a cold and overcast day. The full planning committee were due to consider Brenda Davison's drawings. She had incorporated some of my ideas into the scheme although the scale of the building was much larger than I had anticipated, but nevertheless I genuinely felt that the project would work. The entrance to the church was through a small shopping precinct, consisting of five small lock-up shops and a generous restaurant. In the summer I could visualise parasols over tables and people enjoying the ambience of the scene. This could only happen if the old church were demolished.

The planning meeting was due to start at two o'clock. It was a crowded room we entered, about thirty feet square, with a typical judge's bench and a U-shaped set of tables in front where the councillors were gathered. There were just a couple of seats available for us in the public gallery, we were joined by Philip Ashby, Secretary to the Parochial Church Council. We listened to the opening remarks of the Chairman, warning us not to say anything but to remain silent during the proceedings.

Somehow things seemed to go wrong from the word go. It was obvious to us that the Madam Chairman felt the gravity of the situation. A church like Christ Church in the High Street should not be pulled down, but the whole situation should be given a lot of thought and no precipitous action taken.

After her opening remarks, we went straight to Mr. Watts, an officer of the Council whose job it was to present our case. Everything that followed seemed to go wrong. Acetates had been made of the plans and these featured on a screen. The wrong elevations were put up, and very soon the projector broke down. A lady picked up the machine and walked out of the room. I began to feel that the devil was very much in evidence and seemed to be winning the day. Soon the vote was put, five people voted in favour of our whole scheme going through, six voted against. The Chairman used her vote to reject our plans. I was devastated. I sat there wondering, 'Just where do we go from here?'

The meeting then went on to discuss 'the listing,' (a procedure in English Law whereby historical buildings can be registered as historical monuments and therefore cannot be touched without a ruling from The Department of The Environment). That too, looked as if it was going to be a straight nod of the head from Madam Chairman to list the building, a number of people siding with her. But in quite an amazing way, what happened was, seven people voted for the demolition of the church and three against. This unprecedented step seemed to be largely brought about by the threat of our congregation moving out and leaving a building to be vandalised while we worshiped in the local primary school. I went to see Gerry Plastow, the Town Planner.

'Is it bad news?' he asked.

I replied, 'Yes it is, they have turned our plans down.'

He just looked at the floor for a minute.

'Where do we go from here?' I asked.

'Well, there are three ways open to you. You can appeal and I can give you the documentation and the address to write to. Secondly, the decision may be overturned by the Full Planning Committee. And thirdly, you can re-design the new church within the context of the old, by tastefully modernising the building.'

I suggested to him there was a possibility of going to the Full Council. He rejected that idea. As an example of what can be done, he showed me one or two pictures of what had happened in other places, I came away from the Planning Office at about twenty to four feeling terribly punctured, and I must admit very angry with God. Why had he let us down? It seemed to be the end. I came home, Celia was polishing the staircase and looked at me as I walked through the door.

'Well', she said, 'How did it go?'

I said, 'We lost the day, they kicked our plans out.'

The look on her face dropped, and within a minute she had made a cup of tea and we were sitting at the kitchen table.

She said, 'I could cry.'

I said, 'Well so could I, but that's really not going to answer the problem at the moment.'

I was in a daze, questioning God's whole procedure. If the Lord was not in the vision to begin with then it brought into question my whole calling to Tunbridge Wells. Did God really want me in Tunbridge Wells after all? Was I really here to build a new church? Was I in the right place? I turned to Celia. 'If it means my resignation so the Lord may go and do what he wants to do, I'm prepared to resign'.

Then the thought flashed through my mind — children, education, their home and the other work of the parish. It seemed a nonsense of a statement — I dismissed it almost as quickly as I had thought it. I rang Brenda Davison, she was pretty upset by the outcome.

'Oh dear, dear,' she said, 'Where do we go from here?'

'Well Brenda, right now I feel like throwing in the towel.'

'Oh we can't do that,' she said, 'We'll appeal'.

'O.K.' I said, 'Let's go for it, have you got the name and address and the details to appeal?'

'Yes, I've done this before.'

She was going to contact the Planning Office the following day, and find out exactly the situation. I then rang the Bishop of Tonbridge.

'Oh dear, John', he said, 'What on earth can I say. What a disappointment for you. I feel for you in the situation. Would you like to come over and discuss it?'

'No, no,' I muttered, 'I'm quite happy just to ring around and share the problem and possibly galvanise some more prayer support'.

He remarked that the whole problem of the town centre parishes of Tunbridge Wells had been going on for nigh on eighteen years and perpetually formed part of the agenda of the Pastoral Committee of the Diocese.

I put a call through to Robert Wickham. Robert wasn't in the office, but his secretary was equally devastated by the news, and I left him a note to ring back whenever he could. I then rang Dick Warren, Dick was working in the bank very hard and had had a terrible day, just heaviness of work and pressure, and we agreed that perhaps we should have an evening out and go and sit somewhere and talk about the situation. Stuart Wood got home at 5 pm and popped in to see me and quickly encouraged me that whatever the outcome it was still the Lord's will to go ahead with the new church. He had stood beside me through thick and thin. I felt the loyalty of his churchwardenship.

That night a call came in about quarter to seven. It was a young lady I had led to the Lord some three or four weeks previously.

'Hello, it's Alex here John,' she said. 'I'm doing the Bible studies. I've done the first two. Can you give me a hand with them?'

I thought that at the end of this busy day, what a welcome respite to have some normal parish work to do and escape paperwork, committees and the like. So I went down to see Alex.

On my arrival at the house, she was busy in the kitchen. We sat at the table with her Bible study notes. Within a short while I was playing with her little seven year old daughter, Chloë, and we had prayers together at bedtime.

After visiting Alex and Chloë I went to pay Preben Olsen a visit. He was Chairman of our Fund Raising Committee. As usual a large hand and shiny face greeted me. Preben soon threw away some of the fears that I had arrived with on his doorstep.

'Oh we'll try again, we'll tackle the problem at the council level and lobby some of the councillors.'

This I mused, was Preben at his best. We went through the day's events and I decided to see Jim Perry, the Councillor who did a 'U' turn for us over the listing. We arrived about 10 pm. I told him of our fears and how devastated we felt.

'All is not lost, we've got two or three chances yet to redeem this one, raise the problem at the Full Planning Committee and have the decision reversed, or we could put it before the Full Council, and lastly we could appeal' he comforted.

Wednesday dawned with a frost on the ground, but it was going to be a sunny day. Jessie invited Celia and I to spend lunch with George and Katherine Duncan at her home. I wanted to share some thoughts with them. For many years I had sat under his preaching at the Keswick convention. Now retired, it was a great privilege to have this spiritual giant as company over lunch. Perhaps this was one way the Lord gave Celia and I a measure of comfort. A further tangible measure of support came from St. James's congregation in the form of a cheque for £1,000 and this was soon followed by a similar gift from Edward Hickmott, the local funeral director and someone I counted as a personal friend.

Chapter 4
Consider the ant

Though Celia and I were on holiday in Malta, I was not exactly the best of company at the restaurant. It was large and unfriendly, the waiters fussed around their allotted tables with an air of nonchalance and sometimes indifference. I fidgeted in my seat to attempt to get some measure of comfort. My spinal muscles were in spasm as a result of a diminishing disc which was now squeezing the spinal column. The doctor had said there was little that could be done.

'I carried too many heavy weights in my former job as a Gas Fitter, and slowly crushed my spine in the process,' I had told him.

The pain was now unbearable, I would have to lie down. With apologies to my wife and the English couple sharing our lunch table, I made my painful way to the lift. The cold marble tiles of the hotel floor seemed harder than ever as I made my torturous way along the corridors. With a painful sigh I arrived at our room, and with some difficulty undressed and ran a hot bath, one way I knew of getting a bit of relief. After ten minutes I heard the door open and close and Celia's voice with some concern ask, 'Are you alright darling?'

'Yes,' I offered, 'things will be easier after a hot tub.'

I lay in the water, wondering what the Lord was doing to me, was my ten day holiday going to be plagued by this sort of discomfort? What could benefit my soul by lying here or elsewhere day after day? I checked my growing bitterness.

'Lord you are my father, and you know what I am going through, so I praise you for my pain, and trust that you will have your way with me.'

'Pardon darling?' Celia volunteered, 'I didn't catch what you said.'

'I'm just talking to the Lord,' I replied.

The tiled bathroom bounced the echo of my voice around the walls. Lying in the bath, I suddenly realised that a combination of my hollow back and the shape of the bath caused a suction right where the pain was located. I lifted my spine and the suction pulling on my vertebra gave me immediate relief. I repeated the process about six times. To my relief and thanks to God, the spasm ceased, and I was in a measure of comfort again.

Out of the bathroom I explained to Celia what had occurred, 'Praise the Lord', she smiled. The sun was streaming in through the windows. Still wrapped in a bath towel, I closed the curtains half way and lay on the hard floor with a pillow in the arch of my back; Celia was soon fast asleep snoring on the bed. I began to consider the frustrations that attached themselves to the problem of building a new church.

My head on one side, eyes level with the floor, I noticed an ant, a species I'd always considered placid and industrious but gregarious. This fellow was alone, busying himself with poking the nooks and crannies of the tiled floor. He would first go this way and then that, there seemed no pattern in what he was doing. My ant had made his way to the edge of the carpet. He stopped and seemed to tickle his toes. With a little hesitation, he followed the line up the carpet, then mounted it with a great deal of difficulty, for the carpet pile was like the resistance that pack ice offered to Arctic explorers.

'Go on,' I said in support. 'You can make it'.

The sun was casting the shadows around the room. Soon my ant would be out of the sun and into the cool of the curtain shade. He trundled on and just as I was about to turn over again, I saw that he had found his dinner, a fly, quite dead, but fresh meat and ready for the larder. My ant inspected it, walked around it, stood back and observed it.

'What are you going to do now?' I enquired.

Celia stirred at the sound of my voice, then she turned over and was soon very still again. To my surprise, the ant walked away a few inches. Now what was happening? Was he weighing up the cost of removing the carcass? Was he looking to the horizon for reinforcements? I half imagined the ant cavalry storming over the horizon as some internal intercom summoned them to the task.

He returned to the fly and continued to fuss over it, then, with front feelers gripping the quarry, all six legs leaning backward, his trunk at full stretch, the fly moved ever so slowly. The fly got caught on the carpet. With supreme effort the ant tried first of all to pull to the left, then to the right. Now the ant was on the move again. I felt pleased for him, he was doing a great job. There was the temptation to play God and physically move the carcass a few inches for the struggling insect, but I declined. He needs the victory as much as I do, and some things are wrought better through one's own determination and enterprise. Besides, God must occasionally feel like interfering in his predetermined plan, but resists for fear of spoiling an opportunity for us to learn an abiding lesson.

With a little anxiety, I watched the ant move a large unwieldy package. On the move, he was now making good progress — 'legs to the left and legs to the right, fly makes circle and back to the fight'. It became a dance as the rear end of the ant moved through a full semi-circle to ease the fly out of its tangle. Then all of a sudden he stopped, let go of the fly and wandered off.

'Tea break', I observed with a smile. Or had he given up? Is the job too big for him? It had been a strenuous fight for over fifteen minutes. He stepped off the edge of the carpet and made for the wall below the window. He followed the cranny for some ten inches and without any reason, stopped.

'Harry, you've left your dinner behind,' I ordered. He turned round almost as if he heard me, and made his way back to the fly.

Now with strenuous effort and gigantic pulls, never a push, the fly was moved inch by inch off the carpet and on to the cold marble tiles. Progress now was swift, with no more obstacles in the way, a straight run home and no doubt a cheer of welcome in the fraternity of the ant's nest. Ant and fly disappeared in the wall crevice. He was home, the supreme effort had its reward.

'Consider the ant', I mumbled to myself in a mood of reflection. So you have been given a task, a vision, and brother it's big. What are you going to do? Walk away? It certainly would be a lot easier. After all, look at the terrain ahead, endless committees deliberating and passing resolutions, objectors, like the Civic Society, the Victorian Society, the Historic Buildings and Monuments Commission, the Pastoral Committee of the Diocese, the handful of people in the church, the Diocesan Advisory Committee. The 'pack ice' formed a mighty opposition.

I stood up and sat on the foot of the bed, Celia stirred from her afternoon nap. 'What time is it?' asked Celia.

'Time I tackled the "pack ice" with more guts and enthusiasm!'

Our holiday in Malta was over far too quickly, but as we flew over the island I looked back to the coast where we had been hours earlier. Celia squeezed my hand.

'Alright darling?' she enquired.

'Yep, I'm OK,' I said wistfully. 'It took a holiday, an island and an ant, to help me get things in perspective'.

One thing uppermost in my mind was the safety of the congregation. I had spent many evenings cutting tin squares from biscuit boxes and covering holes in the floors of the church, but what I could not patch up were the great chunks of ceiling falling down near the organ housing. Clearly the building was deteriorating to a point where it was positively dangerous. So, on January 2nd 1989, we moved out of the building into the adjacent church hall. This was just as well, as it was quite clear that progress was going to be long, hard and difficult. The days were dripping by and events regarding the new church seemed to happen more slowly than ever. There would be many days when I would receive, within hours, five encouragements interspersed with five disappointments. One particular night I had made a couple of parish calls and now was in no mood to speak to anyone else. I got into my car and began driving out of town, out of the parish and out of my mind. All I wanted was freedom, freedom from pressure, to escape my home, the church office, to escape the people that pressurised me, to run away from circumstances that needed decisions.

I drove along the Pembury Road, turned right on the old A21, and entered Pembury Village. Up ahead, there was some activity. People coming in and out of the local pub. A garage, brilliantly lit, was advertising cheap petrol. It all looked warm and attractive. I leaned over to my left and read the sign 'Wine Merchants'. I walked into the shop filled with bottles and cans, crisps and bright lights.

'Can I help you sir?' asked the man behind the counter. I gazed around at the kaleidoscope of glass and metal.

'Er, a wine,' I stumbled.

'Red or white sir, dry or sweet?'

I chose a red.

'Carafe or bottle?'

'Carafe.'

I left feeling awkward and guilty, I got back into the car and drove away swiftly towards Hastings. After a mile or two, I came to a junction in the road at a roundabout, and turned right down a country lane. Finding a clearing at the entrance to a field, I parked, switched off the engine and sat quietly in the twilight. From the West, there was a gathering storm. Was this a portent of things to come? Was this some prophetic insight that nature was revealing to me? Was it a rain of refreshing, or something dark and foreboding? I rolled down the car windows and looked up at the stormy sky, my thoughts were confused. Why come out here? For what purpose? I closed my eyes and waited for a comforting voice. None came. I was alone again, empty, lost, confused and desperately lonely. I got out and leant against the car door. I could clearly see the lights of my town glowing on the horizon some three miles away.

I began to cry. For whom? For what? I didn't know, I had no answers. Back in the car time dragged and I became full of self pity. One side of me said, 'Get off your butt end and get things moving in this parish.' Another part of my mind said, 'What the heck. Throw in the towel, it's easier to walk away.'

I got out of the car again and felt the need to talk to God. I was too shot-through with disappointment and guilt. Words came easy.

'Lord I'm tired, tired of the battle, tired of people and their smallness. Lord, I want out, out of the situation, out of the conflict.'

Back came the reply ten feet down in my ear, loud and strong: 'My strength is made perfect in your weakness.'

I lifted my head heavenwards, the night was black. The storm clouds had clearly passed over and now the sky portrayed white diamonds on black velvet. *'The heavens truly declared the glory of God'*. I found myself captivated by the awesome knowledge that God was so great, and I so small! The words of the psalmist came to me: *'What is man that you are so mindful of him.'* The sky looked high. Impossible to touch, and yet it was there. There to look at, enjoy and marvel at but how to reach it? Man in his efforts to touch it floundered on the moon uttering words indescribably puny. I related this scene to the impossibility of raising £2 million, I seemed to be reaching for the universe, and yet I knew God had called me to build a church both bodily as a membership of believers and a building to his glory.

Now it all seemed a long way away. I was lonely and empty of spiritual dynamism. Come Sunday, the congregation would expect a message to encourage, uplift and bless them. Here was I crying over the rough and tumble of a pressing situation. The encouragements would come on a Monday, but by Tuesday afternoon something else would dampen the spirits but... wait for it... Wednesday, the post would give much encouragement yet again... but... hang in there... Thursday looks bleak again! And so it was for months on end, my emotions were pummelled and tossed about. I sat on the bonnet of the car.

'Come on John', I blasted myself, 'You're a man with the gift of faith, and an optimist at that, so stop feeling sorry for yourself and move out.'

With renewed determination, I got back in the car.

'Thank you Lord for that kick up the rear end!"

My strength is made perfect in your weakness, I reminded myself. For a little light relief, I turned on the car radio, when suddenly my window received a tap, tap, tap. I lowered the window, and there stood a lady looking somewhat distressed.

'Can you help me please?'

'What's the problem?'

'My car in these wet conditions has skidded off the road into a very muddy patch of ground. I can't get it out.'

I asked her to step into the car. She hesitated. Noticing this, and the fear behind it, I informed her, 'I am the vicar of Tunbridge Wells, having just stopped for a time of prayer.'

She immediately responded, 'Oh! Praise the Lord, I am a vicar's wife, and truly this meeting is an answer to my prayers.'

Again I asked her to get in the car, which this time she did, having first used two plastic bags to cover her very muddy shoes and ankles. I pulled out of the field and went down the little lane, and there in the sharp headlights was one very forlorn Mini. My immediate thought was to tow it out with a rope, but not finding one, we both went to the abandoned car. I asked her to put the car into reverse, while I would give it a push from the front. That was quite the daftest thing I could have done, for a mini has a front wheel drive, so when she put it in reverse the wheels skidded and I ended up being covered from head to foot in thin, runny mud. I took a step back and took a long look at myself. Gazing out of her front window she observed me, and I was positive that I saw the faintest twitch of her face bordering on a smile!

'We'll abandon that idea!' I called, with not a little mirth in my voice. She switched off the engine and got out of the car. We stood in the darkness.

'I'll flag down the next car,' I reassured her, and after three or four minutes one came down the lane. It had four wheel drive, and was driven by two ladies in their early thirties. Stepping down from the vehicle, they attached ropes to the back of the mini and we pulled it clear.

'You have all been so good. Could I treat you to a little light refreshment at the local hostelry?' the vicar's wife offered. We all accepted, and so got in our cars and made our way to Bells Yew Green. Out of the car, and illuminated by the car park lights, I took a long hard look at my grey clerical suit. A line of mud went up the left leg, and up the left side of my jacket. After a moment of hesitation, I went into the pub, the three ladies in front of me.

The licensee was standing behind the bar next to his wife. He stared at me in amazement.

'Don't even *think* of asking me!' I rounded on him. Within twenty minutes I was on my way home. Now I know God has a sense of humour.

Chapter 5
The long dark night

January 9th 1989 saw the continuation of the weather pattern of the previous few weeks. The New Year had cruised in on a southerly warm breeze and everyone kept saying 'When will winter arrive?' It was the last day of my post Christmas break, so I decided to repair the car (a lady had reversed into me). In the garage, I removed part of the front spoiler with the expertise of a trained mechanic, but all I achieved was the separation of only part of it. Frustrated, I clambered back under the quadrowheel and slowly became more angry at my own stupidity.

'There has to be a way of getting this blooming thing off,' I muttered to myself.

I glanced around the empty garage to see if some mysterious person had crept in and heard me talking to myself. Eventually, after a series of trials and errors with various spanners and bolts, half the spoiler dropped to the floor.

'Eureka!', I muttered, with some measure of relief. 'Now only two more nuts to unscrew and I've cracked this problem.'

Lying on my back in the cramped conditions under the car, neck straining and arms aching, I placed the spanner on the bolt and began to turn it ever so slowly. Without warning the car began to fall upon me as if to crush my head and upper body, and without hesitation I quickly scrambled out from underneath the vehicle. Now the whole garage was rocking up and down as if on some giant cradle. I tried desperately to shake off the awful feeling. I blinked, rather hoping it was something to do with my eyesight; it did not work as an immediate cure. I shook my head to clear the blockage, but the vertigo continued. I was sitting on the garage floor leaning against three cement bags. The feeling persisted. Then I too entered the rocking ship motion, discovering that I could not sit upright. My body keeled over like an overweighted and badly stevedored vessel: the ballast had shifted. Falling on the floor, heart thumping against my ribs, perspiration poured out all over my body, my temperature seemed to fall and rise very quickly, first hot and then cold. With difficulty I staggered to my knees.

'Lord, what is happening to me?' I whispered. I tried to remain calm.

'Now keep calm John, panic will only add to the problem,' I told myself.

The feeling passed over, I sat in the silence, thinking of the family and how they would cope with my sudden departure to glory. Celia would have to vacate the vicarage. Where would she go? Besides, I haven't built the church I was called to construct.

Rising to my feet, legs shaking and hands trembling, I hesitated a little longer, not wanting to move for fear of setting the process off all over again. Whatever it was, the feeling subsided and I regained a little more composure. Staring down at the tools scattered around the car and the parts all over the place, I breathed deeply thinking this would help to stop a racing pulse. I picked up the box spanner, gingerly bent down and slipped under the car, almost as if stalking up to the problem hoping it would not notice my re-emergence as a living and active soul. Within seconds the dizziness started all over again. I gave up, stood up and looked up.

'Where God do I go from here? Who on earth is going to put all that lot together?'

I turned and opened the door to the garage which led up via a staircase to the kitchen, hoping know one would see me. Elaine was on the typewriter in my study, Nicola was in the TV room with Christopher and Kerry. Celia was at work. I sneaked a look at my watch, it was 12:15 pm. Upstairs I lifted the phone. Looking at my hands, I saw that they were wet, cold and clammy. The veins on the back of my hands were knarled, and I reflected on the brown liver marks that told me I was entering that older club of 'sunburned' hands. I rang the surgery, the shake in my voice plus the symptoms I related were enough indication for the receptionist to put me straight through to my doctor, Andrew Macdonald-Brown. His voice was re-assuring.

'What can I do for you John?'

'Andrew,' I said, almost apologetically, 'I don't feel so good.'

I related the symptoms to him and he very quickly replied, 'I'll be there right away, lie down till I come.'

From Nicola's room I could hear the hair dryer whining away. I called to her to come and help me make up our bed. My intention was to lie on the top of the blankets and quietly wait for Andrew. She came in and before she could comment on my condition, I told her I wasn't feeling too good. We began to straighten the bed clothes, but as I bent forward to help her, the whole world started to revolve.

'Nickles, I'm going into a horrible spin again.'

I keeled over on top of the bed. I managed to grab hold of her. Although she was only 17 years of age she was an immediate comfort to me.

'Dad,' she whispered, 'You're frightening me.'

I lay back for just a minute on my left elbow, not wanting to get my head down again for fear of losing consciousness. I heard Nicola call down the stairs, 'Elaine, Elaine, come quick, dad's not well.'

While she was out of the room, my heart was pounding, the world started spinning. I was perspiring again, but this time I felt cold and clammy all over.

'Please Lord, don't let me go out like this.'

Thoughts flashed across my mind like pictures in a slide show. A removal van, the family moving out after my death, the new church rising and the colourful opening ceremony. Elaine announced 'I've phoned the doctor, he's on his way.' Nicola came in with a damp flannel and lovingly wiped my brow. Within minutes the doctor arrived. I was propped up on the bed clad in dirty jeans with very oily hands and, in the words of one onlooker, with a pallor a whiter shade of grey.

Within minutes I was wired up to a machine, and although he made no direct reference to the cardiac tracing, Andrew thought I may have had a heart attack. By now Christopher was in the room asking questions about the tracing and re-assuring me that I would live. The ambulance arrived and I was taken to Kent and Sussex hospital, with Christopher accompanying me. Dr. Jim Walker was in charge of casualty. Jim and Shirley were at one time in charge of the mission hospital that our church supported at Gahini, and here he was examining me. It was comforting to see a familiar face in these unusual surroundings.

Meanwhile, Celia had been informed by the doctor that I was on the way to hospital. Dr Jim called her in, and Jim prayed and we held hands together. The prayer gave me much strength and I thanked God that he was in that place before I had arrived. Jim's prayer was full of love and so was his tone of voice. I found myself about to cry.

'Jim', I whispered quietly, 'I want to cry.'

'You go right ahead brother', he said, 'there's no disgrace in that.'

'Jim,' I said, 'I seem to have been under pressure ever since I was ordained a priest in 1965, but more particularly over the last 6 years or so.'

He interjected, 'Brother John, dear brother John, you need a rest, a break away from it all.'

My tears now flowed freely. I ignored the possibility of casualty sisters and doctors seeing me in such a state. Celia squeezed my hand and she too was crying. Jim walked across to the sink and brought back a paper towel. It felt course and rough on my face as he wiped away my tears, it was done with such tenderness, I very much appreciated the gesture. A picture came to mind, Jesus washing the disciples feet. How tenderly that would have been done.

After blood being taken for testing and answering many questions as to what had happened, I was transferred to a bed trolley and taken to the Intensive Care Unit. A further cardiogram test revealed no signs of a heart attack. The blood samples revealed no abnormalities and my blood pressure was quite acceptable. I was wired up to a machine that recorded my pulse rate. The clock on the wall was approaching 5 pm and I watched the food trays come and go. Two more doctors came to see me and again I repeated the same story to them both. By now it was becoming clear to the medics that in some way my neck was involved. After a lot of note-taking they left. It was 7:15 pm and I had not eaten since 9 am, and that was only two small oranges. I ventured to ask with a little firmness could I eat or did my condition dictate I die of starvation? Hey presto! one cup of luke-warm tea and a sandwich.

The following day I was transferred to ward nine and sister Rica, actually named America, came to see me from the ICU and check that I was comfortable. Within a couple of days I was down at the x-ray department having my neck pictured. The plates came back and I was invited to the ward office to view them with the registrar.

'Well now', he pondered, 'Let's look at these.'

Into the white frame went my neck.

'Aha, that would appear to be your problem.' He pointed to the x-ray plate on the left.

'You have a condition called cervical spondulosis.'

'Does that mean I'm pregnant?' I quizzed

'Cervical means neck,' he responded with mirth.

Thursday came and I was duly discharged. The lads on the ward had been superb and we had had a good deal of humour together. As I was leaving one chap came over to me and said, 'Thanks John for humourous anarchy'. With that I left.

A few days out of hospital I decided that I needed more fresh air than simply sitting out on the patio in a ski jacket. I wandered into the town centre feeling somewhat frail and nervous. I walked into Hammicks bookshop, not looking for anything particular but as books play such an important part in my life it seemed a friendly atmosphere. At one point I lifted my head to look at the shelves, and then it happened. The bookshop began to move like a yacht in a heavy swell. Without appearing to draw attention to myself I grabbed a shelf and just hung on. When not looking at the ceiling the feeling soon passed. I discovered a soreness in the back of my neck. As if walking on ice I went outside and turned left towards the precinct and entered Marks & Spencers. I spotted a friendly face, Paul Plumley, a chaplain to SASFA, a charity supporting servicemen. He naturally asked me how I was and I briefly told him my story. His reply was something on the lines that God requires us to rest and in some cases has to force us to put down the tools of our trade for a while. I found these words a comfort.

I had to plan a proper break away from things so, returning to the house I promptly rang Brenda Davison our architect. As a result of this conversation she was more than willing to put at our disposal her little crofters' cottage in Villa Nova de Milfontes, a small town midway between the Lisbon and the Portuguese Algarve. So it was, Celia and I spent a restful time relaxing and walking, taking the odd meal out eating native. Having hired a little Fiat Panda car which proved very durable during our time in Portugal, we saw much of the coast and hinterland of the country. After two weeks it was time for

Celia to return home, while I would stay on for a further two weeks.

It was still dark as we left the little croft-like villa in the Rua de Avenida Andores, a small quaint street just off the town centre We quietly closed the door with the key and within minutes the little car was chugging its way merrily down the road to Cercal and on to Faro. After an hour or so the sun rose and the stark beauty of southern Portugal appeared as if out of a mist. Soon the *aeroporto* signs came into view, I turned into the car-park and placed the car near the Airport lounge. For a time we sat in the semi-cold under a bandstand like structure and shared niceties, but it was obvious that we were play-acting with each other. We entered the airport complex, and after checking in and a wait that seemed too long, Celia left me and went through the final boarding gate. Walking through the car park, I looked up at the departure lounge window and saw her waving to me. A large lump appeared in my throat and with a sense of British grit, I waved back and drove out of the Airport. Within the hour I was heading back down the same road alone. I could still see Celia in my mind's eye, waving from the upstairs lounge above the booking hall.

The sun was now well up. I made my way along the coast to Albufeira and Lagos. The latter place was so full of colour and people, a fishing port with the high aroma of scents from the sea. I parked the car by the sea wall, smiled at a stationary policeman and crossed the road to the large fish market. The market was the shape of an aeroplane hanger, I made my way in through a large door. Everyone seemed to be dressed in black and all were approximately nine inches shorter than myself. I gazed in a bewildered fashion at the whole range and variety of fish laid out on slabs of marble. The place was crowded, smelly and noisy. I saw an exit door at the far end of this enormous market, and was about to make for it when I stopped and looked up into the huge roof space. The ribbed wooden rafters looked like the empty interior of a ship's hull upside down. All of a sudden I had a terrible dizzy spell. I froze to the spot and grabbed hold of a fish-bench to my left. A horrible feeling of nausea came over me. My legs began to shake and I could feel the blood draining from my face. At that moment I felt desperately alone. No one spoke my language, who would I call upon for help? Surrounded as I was with hundreds of jostling people, I seemed cut off all the more. No amount of chattering and excitement of the fish market seemed of any comfort to me. With not a little trepidation I made for the entrance I had just used, re-crossed the road and sat on the sea wall next to the car. The proximity of the vehicle presented a distinct comfort to me with its happy associations of the previous few hours.

I sat in the car and ate a sandwich Celia had prepared earlier. After a brief walk, I returned, and soon I was on the way to Milfontes via the coast road. Back at the cottage, I spent the evening creating a set of playing cards out of bits of torn paper I found in the writing desk, and listened to the BBC World Service on the radio.

The next thirteen days I spent sunbathing, watering the garden and preparing meals. Most of my evenings I spent in a little café watching Portuguese football with the local builders and fishermen. On one particular evening one of the fisherman treated me to an alcoholic beverage which made the television screen go somewhat blurred and prompted me to make an early exit. I turned right out of the café and after a further couple of turns left and right found myself outside the Police Station. Two armed policemen were leaning against a wall next to a Land Rover.

'*Boa noite.*'

'*Boa noite, Boa noite,*' they replied.

Both appeared mystified as to where I was going. Within twenty-five yards I found myself facing a blank wall, and with some embarrassment, and in almost complete darkness, I studied the architecture. With a swift about-turn, and wondering how I was going to pass the policemen, I simply gave another '*Boa noite*' and made my way back to the villa.

Walking back to the house I felt melancholy and detached. On entry, the hallway was dark and uninviting. Normally I enjoy my own company, chin wagging with the Lord, assessing the past and preparing for the future, but this occasion was markedly different. I was not tired and so went for a shower. The bathroom was tiny, and above the sink was a small cabinet with a fluorescent light. The gas heater was perched in a recess on a shelf.

After a shower I went to bed. The mattress was about three feet from the floor, with cupboards fitted in the space below. On a shelf above the head, lined up like soldiers on parade, were a set of paperback novels. There were about forty in all, ranging from science fiction to thrillers and the odd romance thrown in for good measure.

I ran my finger along the books like a piano keyboard. Nothing of interest. My watch showed 12:50 am. I switched off the lamp above my head, and settled down to sleep.

Thought: You're not tired; this is going to be a long night.

I know I'm not tired but there are ways of getting to sleep. Celia advocates deep breathing.

Thought: That won't work, oxygen is running to your head and waking you up.

It's quiet.

Thought: It's lonely.

It has been a good break for Celia and I.

Thought: She's not here now and you are on your own.

I have the Lord with me.

Thought: God is not tangible and comforting.

'I will never leave you nor forsake you,' he said.

Thought: Where is he now? You're on your own and lonely. Perhaps you're mixed up and God is not bothering with you.

I'm not mixed up and for your information there are twelve angels with drawn swords around my bed right now.

Thought: I'm not disputing the presence of angels, but you must admit that having had dizzy spells you could collapse and no one would find you for quite sometime.

Julio would find me.

Thought: Julio only checks the property long after the holiday makers have left and that could be an awful long time. You're not tired.

I sat upright and switched on the light and checked the time; 1:15 am. I decided to read Psalm 91: '*He who dwells in the shelter of the Most High, who abides in the shadow of the Almighty, will say to the Lord, "My refuge and my fortress; my God in whom I trust".*' I particularly took great comfort in the verse: '*You will not fear the terror of the night, nor the arrow that flies by day, nor the pestilence that stalks in the darkness.*'

'Lord, I'm yours... hold on to me,' I said audibly.

I placed the Bible beside me on the bed. Outside the night stillness was punctured by the rat-tat-tat of a small two-stroke motorbike. There are thousands of these in Portugal, and Milfontes has its fair share. The noise came nearer and I could hear laughter and people talking.

'*Boa Noite!*'

'*Boa Noite!*' came the reply. I hung on every cough of the engine until it was out of earshot. I reached for a Geoffrey Archer novel but, try as I may, I could not get started. I put out the light and snuggled down again.

Thought: You're uncomfortable, your feet are cold.

I turned over and pulled the blankets over my ears as if to muffle the voice of my mind. Now my feet were out of the bed and it irritated me. I lay for a while thinking of Celia. She would be home by now with the family. What on earth was I doing here now? The moments dripped by like sand out of an hour glass. I put on the light again, 1:55 am.

'Why doesn't someone walk past the door of this place?'

I got out of bed and re-made it, this time adding an extra blanket from the bed in the other room. Freshly made it felt different and reasonable, sensible and kind almost inviting. My spirits lifted a little. Lights out.

Thought: Feel better now? The bed is hard. Suppose the doctor was right and you did have a coronary! Listen to your heart now! It may stop at any time. You're entering the dangerous years, fifty three to sixty-five.

I'm fine. But why can't I sleep? A hot drink is required. Light on, check watch, 2:30 am. I went to the kitchen and made a drink of tea. I returned to the bedroom switching off each light. In the hallway a sudden blue flash of electricity momentarily lit up the front door, and at the same time the bedroom light went out. I stood in the darkness, the floor was cold, I was cold, the tea was hot and there was still this aching silence. I groped my way to the bed and paused while my eyes became accustomed to the darkness. I could faintly make out a ledge on which to place my cup. Having fingered for the candle holder on the wall, I took out the candle and walked with hands outstretched back to the living room and into the bathroom. A small flame flickered in the water heater on the wall. I got a light from it and soon I was heading back through the living room, avoiding the chairs. Back in the bedroom, candle in holder I climbed into bed and sat upright. The flickering flame held my attention for a long time. Patterns danced on the walls and ceiling. An irritable motor bike rattled in and out of the candle soliloquy.

Thought: You're not going to make it are you?

Of course I am!

Thought: The new church would cost £2,000,000.

So what? That's chicken feed to the Lord.

Thought: Have you got sufficient faith in God?

I was given faith as a gift from God.

I looked at my watch: 3:15 am. I blew out the candle and cocooned myself in the bed. I listened to my heart beat as it pounded in my ear on the pillow.

'It's getting slower... will I die before this church is built? Suppose it isn't built. How many will take joy in gloating over this crazy clergyman who thought he had a vision from God?'

I was getting cold. 'Lord keep hold of me, Your property is in danger.'

Thought: Your health will not stand up to the pressure. Remember what Jim Ball said recently, 'You have a long way to go John!'

I know in whom I have believed, God will see the vision completed and I have a congregation of fine loving people.

Thought: Have you led them in the right direction? Are you sure of the way you have come? You have spent a lot of money so far, it may be to no avail. You're too weak for the task in hand.

When I am weak, that is when God is strong.

I was perspiring all over, my heart was racing and I felt as if I was loosing my mind. I sat up, glanced at my watch, 3:35 am. I began reciting the 23rd Psalm and came to the verse... *'Though I walk through the valley of the shadow of death, I will fear no evil, for you Lord are with me...'* Silence... Darkness. Time dripped by, 3:45 am.

Thought: You are now a liability to God. He ought to dispense with you. Perhaps you are in the way of progress. Remember Moses, oh! yes! He was a leader and a visionary, but he didn't see the promised land.

If that's what you want Lord, then let it all end now. I am not prepared to go on if I am the obstacle. Take care of Celia and the children for me.

I listened to my heart beat again. It was steady. I tossed and turned, wrestling with myself, the bedclothes, my mind, the building I was in... I drifted off to sleep.

The front door rattled with a heavy knock, I shot a glance at the crack in the shutters. It was daylight. I leaped out of bed and within five strides, opened the door. He stood there, approximately 5'10', grey uniform and a heavy bag on his right shoulder.

'*Correio*,' he said. He handed me a letter. I looked down at the correspondence and wondered why he hadn't posted it through the door. I quickly grabbed his attention and said, '*Non electricidade*', and I pointed to the electric meter alongside the front door.

He indicated that it might be the fuse that had blown and he promptly went off down the road. After a hunt in the living room, I found some fifteen amp fuse wire and began to fix the power failure. While doing the job, with the front door open and the sunshine blazing down on the street on this fresh early morning in southern Portugal, I pondered on my long dark night. Had I also blown a fuse?

After a few enquiries, the local electrician was called and a faulty light over the bathroom cabinet was replaced.

In the afternoon I went up to Maria and Mauricio's home and was invited to stay for an evening meal. Maria, who was in her early twenties, and her brother, in his sixteenth year, were friends of Brenda Davison. The father of the family was a fisherman, and with five children Mum seemed always to be washing and cooking! Their home was complete with chickens running in and out of the house, a stone floor, thick stone walls, and small windows. Maria spoke fluent English, Mauricio struggled somewhat with the language, while Manuel and his wife relied upon their children for translation. Soon a plastic cloth was laid on a table and we sat around, some five of us, the older children having flown the nest. Father still wore his flat cap and had a slight aroma of fish about him. I was amused to see, on the wall, a Sacred Heart picture and below it a small display picture frame in which there were six miniaturised varieties of Scotch Whisky, all covered in dust and obviously for display purposes only. Mum came in carrying a large bowl some 20 inches in diameter, and placed it in the centre of the table. A quick glance showed a mélange of fish, chicken, potatoes, salads. Dishes were brought in and we were each provided with an empty plate. As the guest, I was expected to start first, and with some embarrassment I quizzed Maria for help!

'What now?'

'Help yourself.'

Feeling chivalrous, I invited her to start first!

As the meal progressed, Manuel seemed to be adjusting

something under the table, and my curiosity got the better of me. Moving the plastic table cloth away from my knees, I glanced at the floor below and there was a large enamel bowl, filled with red charcoal embers. It then dawned on me that this was a form of central heating while the meal continued. The table cloth was trapping the warmth around our knees — how ingenious! Soon the evening came to a close and I thanked Manuel and his wife. Having spent my last day cleaning and brushing out the cottage I got to bed about midnight. Waking at 4 am I journeyed back to Faro, watching the dawn slowly break as I journeyed south reflecting on my long dark night, and asked myself the question, 'What was Gethsemane really like?'

Chapter 6
Gold in the fire

I had taken it upon myself to telephone the Bishop to find out the date when the Church Commissioners were meeting to discuss our scheme, and hopefully give us the go-ahead. The phone call was brief. It was going to be the next day, March 22nd 1990. This seemed a long way from the earlier correspondence of December 1987 when the proposal first landed on the desk of the Commissioners.

My one thought at this time was to drum up all the prayer support I could with the limited time available. I started with clergy, Chris Collins at St.John's, Clive Porthouse at Christchurch, Southborough, Norman Norgate at St. James and Stuart Dyas at St. Philip's. Then the two Churchwardens, followed by members of the congregation. All, without exception, were pleased to be informed, and promised faithfully to spend some time in the day praying.

I had planned a period of prayer at the vicarage from 10 am to 4 pm and invited everyone to join us. Lesley, my Churchwarden, said without hesitation that she would get the afternoon off. That left Celia and I to take part of our day off and fetch Russell from his boarding school.

The day was somewhat overcast, though the weather forecast promised fine weather later in the day. We were soon assembled and set to prayer at about 10:20 am. We had before us a photocopy of all the names of the governors listed in the recent Church Commissioners Publication. We prayed for each one in turn, Bishops, Cathedral Canons, Archdeacons and various lay people.

Celia and I drove down to Hurstpierpoint to get Russell. On our return Lesley was reading something from the Bible as she entered the final phase of prayer for the day. It was 4:10 pm and the phone rang. It was John Kain.

'Well! Have we any news John?' he asked.

'No John', I replied with a little resignation in my voice. 'We must be patient! The bishop will ring me when he's ready.'

Friday was a normal day, a bit of office work and a time to have a quiet period getting some extra reading done, and a more lengthy prayer time than usual. The phone rang. It was the local conservative office wanting to know whether I still wanted to meet my Member of Parliament and Attorney General Sir Patrick Mayhew. We were having some difficulties with British Rail concerning a piece of land at the rear of the church, which we wanted to purchase but it was proving a near impossibility, so we would ask Sir Patrick to push them along a bit. After all, we were such a minnow compared with the Channel Tunnel Project! Having arranged a rendezvous with John Kain for 6 pm we arrived at the Conservative Club in time for a 6:15 pm appointment.

'Any news?', blurted out the six-foot-plus Member for Royal Tunbridge Wells as he arrived in reception.

'No', I replied. 'I thought you may know something that I don't'.

The MP went into a large rear room. Within minutes we were with Sir Patrick, who sat directly opposite us. He looked tired.

'Well', he boomed, 'I rang Sir Douglas Lovelock, the First Estate Church Commissioner from Belfast, on Thursday morning, and told him that I personally supported the scheme and mentioned the following points. First, the existing church is an eyesore and a disgrace.'

'And an insult to God,' I interjected.

'And an insult to God,' he repeated. 'Secondly, the town centre parish is a viable unit and there exists a lively congregation full of enthusiasm for the scheme. Thirdly, the new project as planned is a good one and should be given all the encouragement it needs'.

He paused for breath. 'So you've not heard from the Commissioners?'

I replied in the negative.

'Well let's find out from the Bishop. Do you have his number handy?'

After a brief call home and the number given, Sir Patrick rang the bishop. There was no reply. We briefly spoke about the failure of British Rail to respond to our further correspondence and Sir Patrick promised to shake them up a bit.

By Saturday evening I had not heard from Robert or the Bishop and it was beginning to distract me. Just on the stroke of nine I rang Robert Wickham.

'Robert how are things? Do you know anything I don't know?

For the first time ever he was speechless. He took a very deep breath and remained silent. I spoke up. 'Robert is everything alright? I'm sorry if I've called at an awkward moment but I thought...'

He interrupted, 'John, John, this is difficult for me. Yes, I do know the result of the meeting. I happened to bump into someone quite by accident. I do not believe it's the last word on the subject and I do not believe you should be too disturbed.'

I remained silent for a few moments, and pondered the worst scenario. Had we had our project rejected and all was lost? A sickly feeling arose in my stomach, 'Oh! No Lord, I thought I can't take any more disappointment.' Robert continued, 'I think you ought to ring the Bishop now and get his reactions. Please don't go to bed thinking the worst, things are not as bad as they appear.'

For a moment I was stunned. What had gone wrong ? Who was to blame? How were we going to get out of this? I gazed intently at the typewriter cover in front of me; the word Brother was clearly written on it. 'One who keeps closer than a brother,' I thought.

The bishop was obviously working at his desk, the telephone was answered immediately.

'Bishop, John Banner here, I gather you may have some news, I've just been speaking to Robert Wickham and he advised me to ring you.'

Michael was appreciative of Robert's loyalty, and told me that he had bumped into him at the entrance to the home of the Commissioners.

'John', he began with just a tinge of tiredness, 'My heart is heavy, the Commissioners spent a whole hour debating the scheme and I fear that we are not through the problems yet. Such was the debate that it ended up with two resolutions and in one of these the chairman had a casting vote. I must confess that I have slept on the matter for these last two nights and have come to the conclusion that as soon as we hear from them officially, we shall meet and discuss our next strategic move. Perhaps you and I, and if you wish, Robert Wickham and Lesley Farrell, (the Assistant Diocesan Secretary) should discuss the matter.'

'Michael, I remain full of confidence and refuse to be put off by these further delays. I agree that we meet, and thank you for all the encouragement you are to us at Christchurch. Good night and God bless,' I replied.

Celia came into my study and sat down at the desk opposite to me. I related what had happened. The tone of my voice was sufficient to share with her that I was getting very tired of the procrastination.

'Oh, darling,' she sighed with some despair, 'I could weep for you.'

Within the hour, Celia had gone to bed and the house was unbelievably quiet for a change. I sat in the living room.

'O Lord, what more could we have done as a congregation that would have made a difference to the outcome? We have prayed, fasted, worked hard, lobbied, argued our case before historical pressure groups, sent letters to town councillors, attended architectural meetings and so on — why has it failed? Is it me Lord? Would your will be better accomplished without me? Will getting rid of me help the situation?'

With head was in hands, I whispered to God, 'You're in control, Lord.'

On Sunday morning I made my way to the church as usual. It was a bright and beautiful day, but storm clouds were gathering in my heart. How was I going to preach the word of God in the state that I was in? Far better that I turn around and go home. I felt so useless. On the other hand, what self-respecting Christian minister would allow himself to get into this state? After all, I have a God who is mighty to save, and here I fret like a child, not getting his own way, spoilt and now stupidly aggressive.

'Lord, prepare my heart for worship, to praise you in all circumstances,' I prayed.

'I have learned to be content whatever state I am in' (Philippians 4:11).

Now in church, I had to be a bright and breezy minister, obliged to smile, ask people how they were and assure them of my love and concern. Few would detect the heavy heart I held. I refused to be downcast any more. Paul was in worse circumstances than I, and if he could be content, then so would I! Having robed for the service, and with Dick, my Reader, commencing with a word of praise, I was now content that *all things work together for good to those who love the Lord*. Clearly God was in this disappointment, and he was in total control. I was reminded that gold is only refined in the fire, so in that I would rest my case. Our little church hall was packed to capacity and some were forced to stand throughout the service. The opening hymn began: *Hallelujah, sing to Jesus, his the sceptre, his the throne.*

June 5th was a lovely sunny day. I had planned to meet the clergy at the church hall to discuss the new church scheme. I met Jessie Rhind and Doris Burden, who had provided a lunch for my colleagues. Geoffrey Hyder was already in the small hall and we were soon joined by Stuart Dyas, Norman Norgate and John Hurst. Within minutes we were together looking at the model of the new church. I quickly explained the layout of the church and hall. Various questions were asked about seating capacity and the viability of the shops in the present financial climate. I paused, and looked at the assembled group of clergy huddled around this miniature threat to their parishes. Those in the immediate town centre had already made certain noises that a further church building was not necessary in the locality.

My argument was simply that God was building a new kind of church, not so much the people, that would be theologically unique. I was aware that the building of such a church would be by its very nature, shape, complexity and ambience offer to the Christian community such facilities as would hopefully meet all the gifts of God's people. For example, the coffee bar would be open to all, giving those of our congregation with the gift of evangelism a golden opportunity to verbalise their faith.

The Rural Dean spoke: 'Come gentlemen, we must discuss these things.'

We made our way into the small hall for the meeting and arranged four large tables in a rectangle. Only two of us had any paper work;

Stuart Dyas had prepared a paper and I had made some notes to guide my own thoughts.

The reason for our meeting began three week's earlier at the close of the Parsonages Committee Meeting. This was held at St. Nicholas Church, Rochester, and for me this Committee was fulfiling and very satisfying. After the meeting I went to my car. Behind me were the three Archdeacons of the Diocese, Norman Warren (Rochester), Ted Francis (Bromley) and Richard Mason (Tonbridge).

Conscious of the procrastination I had been hearing from various quarters, I challenged each Archdeacon to comment. I found Norman the most direct and lovingly blunt.

'It's a beautiful scheme John. It deserves to succeed and one does not question the vision God has given you. One question I would like to ask you. Do you have the support of your clergy colleagues in Tunbridge Wells?'

I was devastated that such support from my clergy friends could be questioned. I fumbled for words.

'Norman Norgate at St. James with his PCC have sent £1,000 in support of the new church, Chris Collins at St. John's has always been encouraging. I have no reason to believe that my friends are not supporting me now.'

Richard was less forthcoming: 'I've always believed in the scheme and it has had my undivided attention and encouragement. But as you know John, the powers that be are seriously questioning the way forward and we must await the outcome.'

Ted Francis remained silent throughout.

The journey home took well over an hour. I drove slowly and thoughtfully. My mind ran through all the clergy colleagues I knew in the deanery — who was my Judas? Who was working behind the scenes to frustrate the progress? Who was gossiping to whom? How many ears were listening to other things? I felt demoralised and deeply disappointed.

'Lord, what do I do now? Who do I speak to?'

After tea was over, I went into the study and rang Chris Collins. I recounted the afternoon's events to him.

'Why don't you call the Rural Dean and have a meeting?' he suggested.

Within the hour I had fixed a time and venue with Geoffrey

Hyder, the Rural Dean a man in his sixties, greying, thoughtful and slow in deliberation. It was this meeting that we were now holding.

Geoffrey asked me to introduce the subject. I briefly outlined the facts. We had received Planning Permission in October 1986. The Church Commissioners had visited the town and listened to all representations in September last year (1989) and we were awaiting their report. Any day now we expected to hear from the Department of the Environment that the scheme would not be called in for Non-Statutory Public Enquiry. Furthermore, we were well on the way towards having one million pounds and expected further monies to come in from a compulsory purchase order on Crabb Hall. The level of optimism within the congregation was high and it was, at a time like this, that we needed all the support we could get. The Rural Dean broke the silence.

'Now gentlemen, your comments.'

Stuart Dyas was the first to speak, he was followed by Chris Collins who commented, 'I have always supported John in this vision he has had, and I continue to support him. I must, however, admit that the cost of the scheme is daunting and I wonder whether a compromise solution could have been reached, i.e., using what money the Parish has to tone down the size and complexity of the proposals. I realise that this would be hurtful and that going back to the drawing board at this stage could upset the present programme.'

Norman Norgate spoke in favour of the new church. At this point in the meeting John Hurst left to take a funeral. He rang the Rural Dean later to tender his objection to the new church scheme. Brian Gant, vicar of Charles the Martyr, commented that while earlier he saw the new church as superfluous to the town's needs; now bearing in mind the number of churches already in Tunbridge Wells, he considered that the unique ministry the new church would offer the community, would be conducive to the town in general.

A final summing up was needed and the composite mind of the members was required. It was thought that a possible basis for a joint letter to the Bishop take the following line: 'We are very concerned at the length of time being taken to clarify and resolve the situation, and the damage being done, not only to the congregation, but also to the Christian witness in the town. We are prepared to stand with Christ Church, in promoting the continuing existence and growth of the present congregation, also recognising they need a building of their own. Also parish boundaries should be urgently reviewed.'

In Geoffrey's summing up he freely admitted that he had been much exercised in his soul about the scheme in earlier days. He was now of the opinion that the scheme was worthy of his total support.

Two days later the Pastoral Committee of the Diocese met. In the evening of the same day at about 6 pm, Chris Collins rang me to say that as our Deanery Representative on this committee, he had come away from the meeting extremely excited and proud of our Rural Dean. I naturally asked why, having forgotten the timing of things.

'Well', he said, 'He gave an impassioned appeal on your behalf and that of the PCC. What he said came from the heart and with deep conviction. He carried the day John, and the Bishop, who wanted to review the scheme all over again, lost the argument.'

I did not gloat over this vote against my Bishop. He was not only a personal friend but a fine man of God. He said what he felt was right at the time. Two weeks later the Parsonages Committee met on, what we affectionately called, our picnic. Norman Warren shared with me the sterling job that the Rural Dean had done at the recent Pastoral Committee meeting.

'John,' he said with a satisfied smile, 'Geoffrey was a man truly inspired of the Holy Spirit at the recent meeting.'

Chapter 7

The three angels

On Sunday, October 14th 1990, I was the last to leave church after the evening service. A quick glance behind the building told me that no vagrants were sleeping under the trees or in the organ fan housing — a shed behind the church — where, on one occasion, they had lit a fire and the smoke had wafted into the church. On that day Norman Hutchings, a retired clergyman who helped to take extra services in the life of the church, arrived to commence the early 8 am Holy Communion service. He noticed the smoke and decided it was in our interest to let whatever was burning burn. He sent a messenger to the vicarage to announce the good news!

I heard the door bell go at 7:30 am and Celia, being more awake at that hour than myself, got up, put on her dressing gown and went to the front door. Within a few minutes she returned to the bedroom.

'Darling the church is on fire!' she said with some nonchalance and indifference.

I turned over. 'What a blessing that is!'

'Do we call the fire brigade?'

'Do we have to?'

In my mind I could see roaring flames devouring the woodwork, heating the walls, bricks crumbling, the roof alight and all the problems of demolishing the church disappearing in an hour's good fire! Mindful of the danger to anyone who was trapped in the building, I reflected no longer. 'Call the fire brigade.'

Celia rang, announcing with poise and elegance that she thought the church was on fire. She added, 'there is no immediate danger to anyone and could you take your time in dealing with the issue?'

The following day the church sustained a major break-in. Doors were smashed and a usable piano had been destroyed by glue being poured along the full length of the keyboard.

On Tuesday morning I caught the 9:17 am train to London, meeting John Kain at the station. We discussed one of the major hurdles to the scheme which seemed to frighten people at every turn; the cost was looking more formidable every day. In my mind the two million pound cost of the project was within my level of faith and expectancy, given certain savings on numerous items. Robert would be happier with £1.9m, but the Bishop and the Commissioners were fearful of having to find any balance that the church could not meet if the scheme went ahead as planned. Brenda Davison and Graham Reed (Quantity Surveyor), had suggested the meeting in order to fix the contract price and then we could assess the level of savings we would have to make in order to be within the budget price. We had reached a final stage in the presentation of the scheme to the Church Commissioners, approval had been obtained from the Department of the Environment regarding a non-statutory enquiry. It was considered by the Secretary of State and would not need to be considered as a building of historic interest, and therefore permission would be granted for its demolition. This was a major step forward and was encouraging after all the opposition we had received.

Later at the architects office a major difference of view had arisen between Graham Reed, and John Kain. The former wanted to know exactly how much we had to spend, the latter wanted to know what the scheme, designed by Brenda, would cost. As far as the Q.S. was concerned, his building cost, plus fees and extras amounted to £2.7 million. At an earlier meeting at the vicarage we had decided that £2.3 million was a maximum, and that included £200,000 already spent on fees. Various suggestions were made in an attempt to save £300,000 to £400,000. We looked at the cost of the lift — £50,000, then the large triangular window above the communion table possibly another £30,000. What about some furnishings and fittings? Could we save on certain floor coverings or go for something cheaper? Could we save £37,000 on the organ? John was convinced that the building cost was generally too high and there was 'plenty of fat in there'. It was becoming clear that we could not save £300,000 without seriously damaging the scheme. Robert had assured me that he would be in his London office most of the day, so I rang him while we were all around the table. He gave me the impression, by his tone of voice, that our search for funds was going to be very tough indeed. He quoted Maxwell Creasy who, as a good friend of Robert's, had been at one time Managing Director of Metropolitan Estates Property Company (MEPC). He was now working as a partner for Gladdings Secured Contracts, a company that at one point, some two years earlier, desired a partnership with us but was now not willing to advise the company because of the risks of a poor investment in our scheme. The country was in recession, facing a rise in oil prices, a factor directly related to the Gulf crisis, high interest rates within the order of 15%. Inflation hitting 10.9% and many contractors going broke or at best laying off personnel and batting down the hatches for better times to come. The figure placed on the commercial aspect of the scheme (i.e. the shops and the restaurant) at the height of the property boom was in the order of £1.8 million. We would be fortunate now to get £1.2 million and that might prove to be too high, but we should concentrate on getting the scheme down to the barest bones possible. My thoughts were on the wave length of finding alternative funding for the commercial element, and with our own £1,000,000, the full cost of the scheme could be met. After further heated discussion I was becoming irritated by the fact that here was a work of God and it was subjected to man's censorship, and was in danger of becoming a scheme, that when built, would have man's finger print all over it. It would no doubt end up as a 'hotch potch' of unconnected bits and would give no glory to the Lord. I couldn't take it any longer.

'We are going to build the scheme as originally given by God in visionary form to me and I think we should go ahead confident that what God has begun, he will go on to complete,' I said.

After lunch, John and I left Hampstead for Tunbridge Wells.

I've always believed in angels. Perhaps this stems from my work in the realm of deliverance from demonic oppression. Demonic activity, as I understand it, is the presence of Satan's messengers. Angels, therefore, are the bringers of good tidings, they are here to give messages and, at times, appear in physical form. How else would one entertain an angel unawares? Sometimes the arrival of a stranger, and the timing of that appointment seems uncanny and beyond words. It is no coincidence therefore, that when one is at a very low point spiritually, through circumstances very often beyond our control, that God appears to intervene and save the Christian from any further and unnecessary heartache. There were times towards the end of 1990 when my emotions were being played with like the rhythm of a yo-yo. My Bible reading in the morning would be encouraging. The mail would arrive and someone, somewhere, would be objecting to what we were doing by demolishing the old church, and emotionally I would hit a low point. Within the hour a telephone call would confirm that an aspect of the scheme was successful. By lunch the news would tell of another percentage rise in inflation and the building industry would feel the pinch all the more. A phone call in the afternoon would be something positive from the Quantity Surveyor who would have made a saving in the whole scheme. These were times when I felt an inner greyness and a hollow feeling of not being able to cope. God in his infinite sovereignty and wisdom would send a messenger of comfort.

One night about 10 pm the door bell rang. Opening it, I was confronted by a police uniform and the face of a beautiful girl called Melanie. She said she was calling to see how we were. I remembered that I had put it on the police grapevine, that any of the patrol officers were welcome to drop in for a hot drink any time they were passing by, particularly in winter. Ever since my Liverpool days I had a soft spot and a load of sympathy for the police.

Melanie became a family friend. She always enjoyed finding a home from home at the vicarage. She was a Yorkshire lass from Leeds, and spoke with a tinge of the broad northern accent. She was in her twenties, tall and slim, with long dark hair. Over Christmas 1990 she had decided to pay us this visit, and I welcomed her warmly. After a brief stay, and a promise to come for a meal, she left. The timing of Melanie's visits, including this one, have been a rich source of encouragement to me. Many days in my spiritual greyness were touched by her rays of sunlight. Her very warm personality and ready smile had been a great relief when all looked dark and dismal.

Troops were piling in to the Persian Gulf, and ships were blockading the sea lanes to Iraq. Saddam Hussein was refusing to listen to the overtures being made to him to withdraw his troops from Kuwait, and the leaders of the nations were frantic for a peaceful settlement. It was in these troubled times that David Young arrived to see me about the new building project. He was doing a dissertation for his university and as part of the written work, wanted to see the new church scheme in Tunbridge Wells. I had sent him a good deal of paperwork, including the plans, both to enthuse him and to prepare him for our meeting. He arrived on Thursday 3rd January. He was armed with a case and a camera and after a brief chat over coffee, we got down to the work in hand.

I gave him the vision, the background, and some of the difficulties I had encountered on the way. Once or twice he stopped me rambling, 'I cannot take in too much detail, otherwise my thesis will become too large and unwieldy.' I took the hint and encouraged him to ask me questions. Within a matter of minutes we were down at the old derelict church and immediately he began to take photos. I was expecting someone for lunch so hurried him along and we chatted as we journeyed back across the Grove.

When we were in the study, he suddenly said, 'Do you realise that God has given a similar vision to a handful of men like you, who, believe it or not are strategically placed around the country doing similar schemes? Are you aware that you are making changes that are the equivalent of the work done by Wesley and Whitefield in terms of breaking new ground for the church of the twenty-first century. I am in a privileged position not only to know you, but to have been here today. Thank you for the opportunity!'

I was speechless, taken by surprise. I spluttered something that made no sense and felt my cheeks go steadily warm with sheer embarrassment.

Within minutes he had left. I sat down on the stairs in the hall feeling insignificant and humble. Tears were forming in the back of my eyes and suddenly I felt warm and wanted. Jesus was with me right there on the stairs. David's words may very well have been the Lord's word to me. Certainly it was perfect timing. Then I stood up and muttered aloud, 'Me, little ol' me, with the greats of the Christian church. I've never looked at things like that before!'

Some few weeks passed by. I was in the kitchen making a meal for the children. Celia was working three days a week at Burrswood Nursing Home. She usually prepared some dish in advance and all I had to do was put it in the oven. I proceeded to peel a few potatoes when I heard the front door open and shut and looked at the clock on the kitchen wall. It was 3 pm, too early for the children to come home from school. Footsteps approached the kitchen door, I turned around and there was Sally.

'Hi,' she greeted me in that half-singing voice of hers.

With hands wet and apron on I replied similarly. She walked towards me and gave me the biggest hug possible. Sally came to stay with us at the vicarage in the summer of 1989. The year she was with us was truly the most trying year in getting through the various bureaucratic jungles, and there were times when Sally's shining face made a world of difference.

We talked for a while and then she asked me how I was. I could feel myself slipping into a state of hopelessness and any more talk would have had me letting out the hidden fears I had about the project not succeeding. She squeezed my hand and remained silent. In reply to the question I simply passed it over with, 'I'm a survivor.'

In the first week of February, I went to see my Doctor, to assess whether I was a survivor or not. Going to doctors is not my favourite hobby, after all they may discover that you have something that you didn't think you had, and that disease may be incurable. I arrived at 5:50 pm and proceeded to relate the earlier months to him. I had had my moments of depression but I had always come through them. He was not convinced and proceeded to test my blood pressure and take a sample of blood. I told him that St. Thomas's hospital in London had referred me to a dietician at Pembury hospital. Andrew asked how I was, adding, 'You do know that you have been clinically depressed for over a year.'

I agreed that there were many days in a week when I felt cold and grey inside and no amount of Christian clichés from well meaning friends could help the situation.

'When did you last have a sabbatical leave?'

'I have not had one in twenty six years of ministry, and right now would not thank you for one, soon we shall be under way with the new church and I shall need to be around for all sorts of legal papers to come my way,' I said with some irritation.

There was a hard silence as he agitated with his pen, half wondering where the conversation would go next. I looked at the ceiling and attempted to look oblivious to the situation. He interjected, 'I will not be responsible for your health if things do not happen this year, you cannot go on shouldering this heavy responsibility much longer'.

I felt my cheeks going red. Andrew had never been this straight with me before.

'I'm seeing the Bishop next Monday and will be reporting to him the latest news regarding the scheme,' I said.

He immediately interrupted: 'I will give my total backing to any suggestion that you take a holiday immediately, preferably a planned sabbatical. Your blood pressure is up slightly and I know what is happening, your arteries are furring up.'

I fingered the swab he had given me with an element of nervousness. Outside the surgery I felt depressed. That visit did not help at all, and if anything I should go back in and take him up on the suggestion that a course of anti-depressants would help.

At home Celia asked about my visit to the doctor. I gave her the briefest outline by stating that Andrew had read the riot act to me. I admitted that the one thing that was pressing upon me was the fact that the Borough Council planning permission, which is only given for five years, was now running out.

I pondered: things were going to continue the way they were for some time. There was an increasing difference of opinion between John Kain and Robert Wickham. John was of the opinion that with planning permission running out, we should re-apply in the hope that no alterations to the existing plans need be made. Robert wanted preliminary work to commence on site, for example the digging of some earth works as proof of commencement of the building contract. For my part, I was quite prepared to leave well enough alone. Would the officials of the council want to come and inspect the site?

My mind went back to the first application that we made and the work involved in lobbying councillors, corresponding with Town Planning Officials and endless discussions on the design of the building and its place within the overall town scape. The questions came to mind fast and furious, should I lobby again? Should I write to all the councillors individually? Should I speak to the Chairman of Western Area Plans Sub-Committee? I was not high on enthusiasm.

It had been a trying few weeks. Everything I attempted proved either fruitless or counter-productive. Even visiting a number of people in my parish had proved 99% unresponsive. When presenting the Good News of Jesus to a number of folk, only one girl had responded! She accepted Jesus, and promised to come to church; but as yet had not turned up. As part of our morning service we had anointed a number of sick people and none seem to respond, indeed one positively got worse. We had been praying for six years, fasting on occasions and more recently had held four half-nights of prayer. I expected things to happen... I was disappointed with God, and nothing short of a major miracle would help me come to terms with these disappointments.

'What am I doing wrong, Lord?' I pleaded.

One recent news item had reported that 100,000 workers in the construction industry would be laid off within a matter of days. Surely this was the time, if ever, to get a good price for the building contract. The recession was now biting hard and interest rates were still too high for everyone's comfort. The boom in property prices had stopped, indeed there were signs of a quick tumble and investment in this area was becoming decidedly risky. What would that do to the proposed shopping precinct we had planned with five shops and a restaurant? Finding an investment partner was getting increasingly more difficult. John kept talking about Gulf oil money at no interest. But this was not a serious alternative to sound British investment.

To reach our goal of two million pounds we needed a partner more than ever. Added to this problem I wondered if there would even be any building industry left by the time we went out to tender! To make matters worse on 18th February I received a letter from Robert, suggesting that part of the works for meeting the deadline for the Planning Approval should be to demolish the church hall. This would have undoubtedly been very obvious work on site. John Kain and Dick Warren, however, were not in favour of this. It would mean increasing costs in having to rent the school hall where we were due to spend our sojourn between buildings. I took it upon myself to ring David Goodwin, one of the secretaries at the Church Commissioners. Together on the phone we sorted out some appropriate dates. With the best will in the world we could not get through the Diocesan Pastoral Committee, the Board of Finance, The Pastoral Sub-Committee of the Commissioners, The Full Board of the Commissioners, The Privy Council and a signature from the Queen inside the allotted time. Indeed we would be a good three months beyond the Planning Permission date of October 28th.

June 4th saw the famous evangelist, Billy Graham, appearing at the Celtic Park Stadium in Glasgow for the Live Link Crusade. From there a link would beam down the evangelist's message from a satellite positioned in the sky roughly 24,000 miles above Gabon in West Africa. Within one third of a second the message would be received by the satellite dish on the roof of the Tunbridge Wells Baptist Church. As the Chairman and Billy Graham 'stand in' on the night, it was my responsibility to make the invitation to people to 'come forward' on each occasion and receive Christ as Saviour and Lord of their lives. Each night it was thrilling to see so many come into a living faith. All this was a welcome break from the tedium of paperwork, frustrating meetings, and abortive phone calls.

Our small church fellowship was undertaking a colossal and faithful enterprise. God had given the vision, the money was coming in from the congregation, now approximately £200,000, and with earlier investment and interest rates very high, the fund was nearing £800,000. Such sacrificial giving from the congregation was most encouraging.

I reflected that the timing of God was truly perfect for our new church. I had a deep sense that God ultimately was in control.

Chapter 8
Haggai's word

I was quite determined that this year I would not be caught out, and I was going to get my beans in early. I went down to the boiler room much to my surprise and delight, eleven of the twelve beans were now a stringy nine inches tall. I carried the beans down to the garden. Having previously trenched and manured the earth, I took the beans out of the pots and lovingly set them in a row. It was a beautiful Spring day, 9th April, 1992. Although it was a Thursday, I felt I had too much on to take the whole day off. Miles was off school and, as I struggled with my bean poles, he wrestled with the lawn mower.

Back in the house, I made a coffee and sat out on the rear patio, the sun trap and the warmth gave me a feeling that God's love was still there, despite my many periods of coldness. The words of the hymn came back to me as I sat in the sun, 'And those who fein would serve him best, are conscious most of wrong within'. I continued my pattern of thought — 'Why can't I be a better Christian, why can't I be a better prayer?' One pastor in Korea was quoted in a recent Christian newspaper as saying, 'Any pastor worth his salt should spend at least three hours in prayer every day'.

Tomorrow would be a big red letter day as regards the new church. All the tender prices would be in from eight major contractors, and we were to meet in the offices of John Kain. I was so thankful to God that we had reached this stage that I had called the congregation to prayer every evening of this week. At the end of the first night of prayer we finished at 9:45 pm. After a brief, 'thank you' and 'goodnight' I left the vicarage and went down to church. What could we salvage? After a brief look round the only things worth saving were our Communion table and new chairs which would be stored in the Porto-cabin which was housed at Pym and Ian's place in Wadhurst.

I made my way into the small hall. Piled against one wall were a dozen or so delightful children's spindle chairs. One lady had offered forty pounds for one of these, so they were well worth keeping. In the kitchen was a small domestic fridge, showing signs of rust. This reminded me of more than one occasion when people with a good heart, and the best intentions, would offer the church of God their old appliance because they had bought a new one. Over the years I have been offered pots, pans, crockery, carpets, lampshades and the like and all because: 'Would you like our old one, we have bought a new?"

What makes people put their priorities the wrong way round? A quick glance at 2 Chronicles 1-3 would soon reveal that God at all times would have the very best, and the book of Haggai is unequivocal in its demand that God's house should take priority over our own:

> *'This is what the Lord Almighty says: "These people say, 'The time has not yet come for the Lord's house to be built.'" Then the word of the Lord came through the prophet Haggai: "Is it a time for you yourselves to be living in your panelled houses, while this house remains a ruin?" Now this is what the Lord Almighty says: "Give careful thought to your ways. You have planted much, but have harvested little. You eat, but never have enough. You drink, but never have your fill. You put on clothes, but are not warm. You earn wages, only to put them in a purse with holes in it." This is what the Lord Almighty says: "Give careful thought to your ways. Go up into the mountains and bring down timber and build the house, so that I may take pleasure in it and be honoured," says the Lord.'* (Haggai 1:2-8, NIV)

Faced with the prospect of opening the tender documents the following day, I had to reassure myself that I would not be concerned. Faith and a clear understanding of the will of God would see the new building rise in the High Street. After all, many had been the moments when anxiety would flood the soul. The thoughts of failure rattled through my brain, such as: 'Was the Liverpool vision a trick of the Devil? Did I neither see nor hear a messenger from God? Was this an apparition conjured up by a vivid imagination? At twenty past midnight was it the result of a tired mind at the end of a long day?'

I confronted the facts. Close to £350,000 already spent. A congregation expectant of a new church, and having raised some £200,000 pounds from a couple of hundred people, how would I explain that their money had been spent on an abortive attempt to build a new church? In the darkness I reassured myself that all these were natural thoughts of an ordinary human being. Concerned as I was for the ultimate glory of God, and that the new building should make a clear statement that 'God is not dead', and all the encouragement that this would give to vicars and pastors languishing under a heavy burden of an historical building which could not be changed, others would no doubt be faced with similar situations in the future.

Seeing the new church as a result of the demolition of an old building in the Victorian Borough of Royal Tunbridge Wells, would surely encourage many to take the initiative, after all, how many historical church buildings were there in some of our Victorian town centres, and how many of my colleagues would love to see change, or reordering of their church and, in some cases demolition and re-building!

In the nervous hesitancy of these days, was I in good company like the prophets of old who, with a great venture to accomplish for God, found themselves at times, personally fearful of failure? I concluded that under the circumstances my feelings were both normal and natural.

April 10th drifted in upon a warm southerly breeze. It marked the culmination of fourteen years of waiting to see the new church prices from the major contractors. John Kain had told me that fifty-seven contractors were anxious to build the new church, and over the intervening weeks, we had sat in the architect's office winnowing down the numbers. First to thirty, and then to fourteen, and then to an agreed eight. At twelve noon, after prayer, we would open the envelopes, asking God to gives us his guidance to choose the right contractor.

In fairly cramped conditions in the offices of Joyes & Co., we sat around a green beige table. Sitting to my right was Graham Reed. He had a large pad open in front of him having listed the main building contractors. The column headings he had at the top were obviously concerned with price and length of contract, plus any variations. On his right hand side sat Brenda looking quite relaxed, and dressed in blue. She too had a pad in front of her. To Brenda's right sat Dick

Warren. At the far end of the table was John Kain. In front of him were eight large envelopes, he had in his right hand a standard office letter opener. To my left sat my two Churchwardens, Lesley Still and Simon Bannister.

I took it upon myself to chair the meeting.

'I suggest, Ladies and Gentleman that we begin with a prayer, bearing in mind the importance of our meeting and seeking God's guidance on the right contractor for our new church scheme.'

After prayer I shot a glance at Graham Reed, who smiled, and in that smile there was a belief that what we were doing was right before God.

'John would you be kind enough to open the envelopes?' I asked.

He took the top envelope off the pile and carefully opened the contents. No one said a word. Somewhat nervously I asked, 'Which contractor is this?'

'Wiltshire', John announced. One could see his eyes quickly scanning the pages. He then announced the figure.

'£3,047,377.'

I positively felt my heart beat increase. I shot a glance at Dick Warren, there was a distinct look of worry on his face. Graham, Brenda and the two wardens remained quiet. John proceeded to open the second envelope.

'Croudace,' he announced. His eyes scanned the letter. Lesley shot a glance in my direction. Her face was totally expressionless.

The figure was announced, '£2,991,924.'

My thoughts went back to Robert Wickham as he pleaded with us to keep the contract to £1,800,000. We were obviously going to be well outside that price. Graham muttered something about contract period and John, with a further glance at the letter, announced eighty-eight weeks.

'And... Wiltshires?' enquired Graham.

John replied, 'Sixty-five weeks.'

The third envelope was opened and he announced the figure before the contractors name. Three of us chorused, 'Which contractor?'

'Mowlem,' said John and then stated the figure, '£3,193,987 — with a contract period of ninety weeks.'

At this point Dick attempted to lighten the proceedings with the remark: 'Anyone got a spare million they don't need?'

Lesley looked at me. 'Remember the text of scripture last night?' she said, 'It was a quotation from 2 Chronicles 7:14-16.'

It started to run through my mind: *'If my people who are called by my name humble themselves, and pray and seek my face, and turn from their wicked ways, then I will hear from heaven, and will forgive their sin and heal their land. Now my eyes will be open and my ears attentive to the prayer that is made in this place'*. I mused over the text. This was God's promise to Solomon, after his prayer of dedication of the building of the new temple.

'Wimpey,' John announced, '£2,799,571.'

'And the contract period John?' said Graham Reed.

'Seventy-four weeks.'

The next contractor was Longley, £2,799,947, with a contract period of sixty-seven weeks, with a reduction of £102,326 if concrete were brought in by Readymix. Then Balfour Beatty at £2,847,735 and a contract period of sixty-three weeks. When Pearce Construction price was read out, John followed with the words, 'They don't want the work.' The price was £3,247,436 with a contract period of seventy-four weeks. The final contractor was named as Waites and the price at £2,893,812, with a contract period of seventy-six weeks.

Everyone relaxed physically and leaned back in their chairs. John Kain seemed bright and encouraged and remarked on how near some of the figures were.

'Well, we asked for a Rolls Royce, now we have got to settle for something less'.

Graham Reed interrupted John, 'I am pleasantly surprised', he said, 'I expected the figures to be much nearer three and a half million. Quite a number of the contractors rang me in the office and were having some difficulty in pricing this job'.

I then spoke up, 'What is the procedure from this point on?'

Graham commented, 'I take the documents home and carefully go through the paperwork.' Looking down at his notes he continued, 'I shall look at the following... Wimpey, Longley, Balfour Beatty, Waites and Croudace and I shall report to John Kain in the first instance, within a few days after Easter'. I turned the pages in my diary and this would take us to April 21st.

There followed a discussion concerning the roof design, and also the structural engineer's insistence that concrete be mixed on site. In a few of the contract prices there was a considerable discount if concrete were brought in 'ready-mixed.' Graham Reed opened another enquiry as to the exact budget price we should work to. I responded, 'I believe £2,000,000 has to be the deadline and if my arithmetic is right, the Parochial Church Council can commit £1.2 million. Robert Wickham, I believe, will gain a further a £250,000 from the District Valuation Officers agreed settlement concerning the compulsory purchase order on Crabb Hall, and I do believe the Diocese will invest £3-400,000. The remaining £300,000 should be found from city investment money.'

I glanced at the clock. We had been together an hour and twenty minutes, and my stomach was announcing every two minutes that it was time for lunch. We gathered up our papers. Graham piled the Tender Documents into a large case, and I suggested that we would go down to the Calverley Hotel and have a nice meal. I couldn't get over the air of confidence that seemed to exude from all of us and I can only think that, with so much confidence and faith in God, the building would soon rise in the High Street to his praise and glory!

On April 13th I rang Robert Wickham and gave him the contract prices. Once or twice Robert interjected in order to check the precise figure. I finished and waited for him to make some response.

'John, we have got to make savings. I can live with £1.8 million and I can tolerate £1.95 million with some difficulty, but £2 million plus is a psychologically bad figure, and we may have trouble in raising this extra amount.'

I reassured him that we had asked for a Rolls Royce and must now be satisfied with a Ford Granada. There were savings we could make and this we would proceed to do.

April 16th was Maundy Thursday, and on this day every year the Bishop summoned all his clergy to the Cathedral in Rochester. The occasion was for fellowship with one another in the context of a Holy Communion Service, and at some point we would reaffirm our Ordination vows.

The service commenced with the opening bars of 'Oh! Praise ye the Lord, praise him in the height...' Then began the colourful procession as senior diocesan clerics made their way up to the

Chancel. I noticed Colin Buchanan, now an Assistant Bishop in the diocese and Vicar of St. Marks, Gillingham. Next to him stood Bill Flag, another Assistant Bishop and General Secretary of the South American Missionary Society. And there, coming up behind, was the familiar figure of the former Bishop of the Diocese, The Right Rev. David Say.

After a further hymn, the retired bishop took to the pulpit. He was a mountain of a man, in height all of six foot five inches and weighing some eighteen stone. He possessed a voluminous voice, and he challenged the assembled clergy to rise to the needs of our day.

The service over, Chris Collins and I dis-robed, climbed the steps from the Crypt, and there at the top of the steps stood David Say. Now in his seventies, he was shaking the hand of each man and women. He saw me and immediately he voiced, 'And how is the new church going John?'

His eyes peered down, expectant, confident and encouraging. I immediately rose to the challenge of a firm hand shake and replied with a practical assertion.

'Well, Bishop, we have just opened the contractual prices and after making a few economies, we shall appoint the builder.'

He boomed back, 'Well done! Keep pressing forward and let me know how you proceed.'

Over the nine years I had spent in the parish, a true estimate of my time devoted to the congregation and parish, together with the planning and rebuilding of the new church, was something I had to learn to keep in proportion. A number of the senior Christians would always remind me, and quite rightly so, that people mattered more than things.

Partly in response to the challenge of the future, I wanted the congregation to come together over a weekend to get to know each other intimately, and also to plan and set goals for the years ahead. So the weekend after Easter, some thirty-six of us went off to Pilgrim Hall situated near Uckfield in East Sussex. We split into four groups: Adults Meetings, Youth & Sunday School, Worship and Evangelism. I gave two addresses on church growth, and it was quite obvious in the early stages of the conference that there were two of the four areas of growth in which we were well accomplished. Firstly in qualitative growth, that is the years of praying and fasting responding to sermons and attending Bible studies, which had seen our Christians reach a high standard of quality. Secondly, in the area of organic growth, during which we had wept and loved and shared together. We had cared deeply for one another, sharing our wealth and goods, we had lived with disappointments and now the reality of this organic growth was beginning to dawn upon us. Numerical growth had suffered, but this could be attributed to a number of factors. First, we had left our large Victorian church and conducted our services in the small hall adjacent to the church building. This move, having a low profile, now prevented the usual ten per cent from coming into the church. Meanwhile others were leaving for pastures new so our numbers dropped considerably. To many people, the church had closed and the congregation scattered, and this prevented any further interest as so many were led to worship elsewhere. Secondly, we could not use our church hall for extra activities, for example, uniformed organisations, meetings for the community, such as Women's Institute and general hire of the premises for such things as receptions and nursery groups. Thirdly, some members of the church who could not tolerate worship in the cramped conditions of the hall, and with the distinct absence of the stained glass windows, brass and the pipe organ, promptly left to worship elsewhere.

The results of the weekend turned out to be a great success. Much lateral thinking, brain storming, crazy ideas and revolutionary thoughts, all disturbed the status quo, and gave us a fresh look at ourselves and the patch of ground in which God had placed us.

Back at the vicarage Dick phoned to say that Jim Ball, who had been a Reader at a local church, had died. I remembered Jim with much affection, for many were the dark days, heavy with greyness and my emotions punch-drunk, that I would turn to him and share my innermost thoughts, fears and anxieties. I thanked God for Jim, and pressed on with the work in hand.

Celia and her mother were visiting our daughter Nicola in Brisbane, Australia, whilst I was left looking after the two youngest children. Cooking is not my greatest attribute, and I must admit that one reaches the precipice of one's knowledge at times. Some years ago I was left supervising the children in Liverpool and began to cook Sunday lunch. I boldly went where I had never gone before. Leg of lamb in the oven, sprouts in the pan, carrots peeled and diced, potatoes boiled and then placed in the deep fat for crispness. All was going well until I came horribly face to face with what turned out to be my Waterloo. The gravy! Help! How do I make gravy? Water in the pan, gravy browning to follow. What next? It looks too watery, so I thought, 'I know — baking powder is supposed to thicken things up'. Thus added, the children and I waited for the concoction to cook. Then to our horror, out from the pan appeared the largest white balloon, growing all the time — we remained speechless till my curiosity came to the rescue and I poked the balloon with a fork! So ended my attempt at gravy.

In early May the 'Four Just Men' were continuing to find ways and means to raise more money, but the world's economic climate was becoming more gloomy by the day. The High Street in Tunbridge Wells, at one point, had ten shop premises empty. The building industry had it's back to the wall and new building schemes were few and far between. Investment in property was looking less likely to make a better return than monies deposited in an ordinary bank account.

I decided to call a meeting, having been given the prospect of a town centre doctor being interested in having a health centre in the new precinct. I was now becoming accustomed to setting out the table in the living room for yet another meeting. This was to meet the doctor concerned and see if it were feasible for his surgery to be situated in the High Street. John Kain arrived, accompanied by Robert and Dick. Robert reported that there had been a possibility of a rich young cleric coming into a goodly inheritance who may be interested in placing some finance into the precinct, but this line of enquiry did not bear fruit.

'We'll just have to find the money elsewhere' said John Kain.

I didn't feel at all depressed, I wanted to encourage the progress of any negotiations that had already begun, or indeed were promised.

'The bigger the problem, the more glory to God', I said with great determination.

Dick Warren interjected, 'Now we are into a "water on the sacrifice at Carmel" situation!'

The worst scenario can only enhance God's glory.

'Well Dick, man's extremity is Gods possibility', I replied, and with that we proceeded onto other business.

Robert reported on one or two enquiries he was making with a local retailers. I added to this that an initial enquiry was coming from a Christian printer and there was some hope that he would take one of the units. Within the hour, we met the doctor and talked at great length about the possibility of setting up a health centre within the precinct. After the doctor left we continued our meeting, focusing our attention on the lack of progress concerning the District Valuation Officer's financial judication over the Crabb Hall settlement. Robert admitted quite freely that he was losing patience, weekly phone calls and letters were not producing the required result.

'The District Valuation Officer is an independent person, paid by the Inland Revenue, stating in his professional judgement what the compensation cost should be and the parties should act accordingly, and if that means the town council must pay a further £200,000, then so be it. I shall not accept anything less,' Robert summarised.

On another issue John Kain was quite clear in his own mind that there was plenty of money available. 'I could get gulf money from the oil rich states tomorrow morning, and if you have no objections to Islamic money, then we can bridge the gap between building and selling off the units by this particular means.'

'John, the Diocese will not allow us to speculate or take any risks', Dick cautioned.

The time was heading up for 7:30 pm and at some risk I threw in a controversial point. I suggested that we approach the builder Oliver Longley, with a view to a private discussion in which he may see some savings, and therefore make it possible to build the church without necessarily going out to tender. John immediately interrupted.

'You know I have been opposed to this particular way forward, once the contractor is participating in the financial side of the building contract, then all sorts of complications arise not least, what is the value of their portion of the contract, and what happens if there is a dispute over certain things?'

Robert intervened, 'We can't see the difficulties you can see John, and obviously we bow to your superior experience in this particular field; but talking to a contractor is not quite the same as giving him the contract'.

Dick followed on, 'It makes sense to me John, and possibly Oliver Longley may see savings that could be made if we allowed his architect to look at our drawings.'

John was increasingly more irritated, so I decided to round off the discussion.

'Let us say', I started, 'that we meet the contractors who had submitted the lowest three tenders. We could pick a nice room at the Calverley Hotel, discuss our situation and see which contractor would be the most amenable.'

At this point John nodded with some approval, and so on that note of agreement we ended our meeting with prayer.

Chapter 9

I caught four fish today

Just a few days before our annual holiday in August I received a letter from Michael, our Bishop. I had written to him a week or so earlier asking to use his name on the Council of Reference for the new church. We were about to reprint the letterheads and as a matter of courtesy we wished to include his name. In his reply, he requested a delay in the printing and made it clear that, in the Autumn, he would be meeting the Chairman of the Diocesan Board of Finance and representatives of the Church Commissioners Pastoral Committee and also the Diocesan Glebe Surveyor, Mr. Robert Wickham. I was alarmed at the use of the words in the Bishop's letter, 'we have reached crunch time'. Two factors were mentioned in his letter and these were of some concern. The first was that my fellow clergy were concerned for my well-being, and the second was the deteriorating economic situation. The implication here was that we would never see the scheme as planned. The Bishop expressed the desire to see me in September. Putting all these points together, I was made fully aware that I would have to answer to him for all the procrastination concerning the delays to the demolition and rebuilding of Christ Church. Right before a holiday, I did not need this letter! It seemed to me that a more helpful line from the Bishop would have been to understand the delays were not of our own making, and that to build a scheme of such magnitude required time and patience. Above all, I personally wanted a ton of encouragement from him, but seemed only to be under increasing pressure to perform.

August 3rd was the first day of our three weeks away. Much of the morning was spent packing our cases and preparing the caravan with all the necessary things. With the caravan packed, and the house left in the capable hands of our older children, Celia and I, with Miles and Kerry, set off for our holiday. I tried to push the Bishop's letter to the back of my mind.

We had booked a caravan site at Blandford Forum, some sixteen miles north-east of Dorchester, in the lovely county of Dorset. The site was down a country lane, set in a lovely valley. After supper I took a short walk around the perimeter of the field. It was getting dark, and my thoughts turned to the Bishop's letter. Try as I may, it was obvious it was bugging my system. My mind flooded with all sorts of questions and, not least, a little confusion about the future and what it held for me and for the family. Would the bishop suggest that Celia and I move to another parish? Or would he simply ask us to build with what money we had in the bank? Why did he not suggest that the delays were part of the plan of God and that we should have to be patient? Our future in Tunbridge Wells could not be torpedoed by the Church of England's system of appointing it's vicars. We would not be obliged to move because the house in which we lived was ours by act of Parliament, and we therefore could stay as long as our age and moral standing permitted. With a million pounds in the bank we could build a most impressive church, and I had to constantly remind people that that was very much a second option with which I would have nothing to do.

Back at the caravan, I went back to the Thursday evening prior to our holiday when Chris Collins had paid us a visit. He had informed us that the bishop had offered him another parish and he had accepted it. Knowing how long I had laboured over the building of the new church, he suggested that it was not necessary for me to build it. After all, I had raised the money, and now it was up to the next man to set in motion the works programme. He cited Moses as the man who brought the children of Israel through the wilderness, but was not chosen to enter the promised land. I reminded Chris that I was called to build the church both physically as a building and as a people. When that task was complete I would seek the guidance of the Lord regarding my future. Naturally I would like to enjoy the new facilities for a few years, but that was a matter too far ahead to see.

After two nights we set off for our next site, some five miles from Okehampton, a picturesque town twenty three miles west of Exeter.

We were now in the county of Devon, the home of cream teas. It was obvious from the dark grey cloud on the horizon that we were in for a very wet time. As expected, the weather closed in and it rained. Between showers the sun gave us little relief, and on one of these rare occasions I sat outside our caravan. The idea was to read the newspaper, but my thoughts soon turned to other things.

I reflected on the meeting we had with the architect and quantity surveyor on July 29th. It was a gloomy affair. We all agreed that the financial climate had changed drastically since the scheme first saw the light of day on Brenda's drawing board some nine years earlier. Most businesses were suffering a double blow, the high interest rates and a local tax known as the Uniform Business Rate. This tax rose sharply and without much warning. Many shop keepers were finding it too much and simply gave up trading. A further burden had been created by the banks' own policy in the late eighties. They had loaned billions of pounds to South American countries, and they had lost a lot of it. Bank charges were rocketing as they sought to recoup the same by charging the UK sector enormous fees for banking. Added to this was the Poll Tax, and for countless thousands of people these sums were as high as £500 a year.

What a time to build a new shopping precinct! Just about everything was against us! Debate with the architect ranged from staying with the plans the way they were and sitting out the recession for a year or two, to phasing down the size of the scheme, pulling the building forward, and making do with an outside car-park behind the church building. We had agreed that the Quantity Surveyor should do a simple costing on likely revisions to the whole scheme. This ran much against the grain for me. As we had prayed long and hard over all the drawings and all the meetings, now it looked as if we were changing our minds in mid-stream. Were we admitting God had led us astray, or had we not heard clearly enough? I could not accept either option.

I decided to call a meeting of the 'Four Just Men'. We had done this so many times before, but now there was a distinct atmosphere of despondency. We had all run out of new ways to launch the financial package needed to prove the scheme was viable. We were soon around the table and into our usual deliberations. I opened the proceedings with prayer, and immediately beseeched God to meet us in our need. To put it bluntly we were all short of ideas, but this gave an air of relief, and for a few moments we simply brain-stormed. One redeeming feature was the fact that we all knew that we had one million pounds in the bank, earning good interest!

'Tea up!' Celia's voice brought me back into the present and I suddenly realised, sitting in my deckchair that the sun was going down and I was getting cold.

The rest of the holiday was taken up with dodging showers and attempting to find new card games as we sat in the caravan. The beginning of the second week of our holidays found us at St. Mawes at the commencement of the Regatta. We had left the caravan at Celia's sister's house. Celia had the opportunity to sail with her cousin Mark, with whom we stayed, and for her, this was the highlight of her holiday. With borrowed wellies, sou'wester and life jacket, she and Mark set off in a force seven gale. I must admit my imagination played havoc with me. With my wife drowned, how would I cope with the parish, the cooking and the kids? I would have to find another wife very soon! Mark's house was an 'up-side-down' affair overlooking the tiny harbour. The living room/dining room was situated upstairs. The bedrooms were below. There was a small wooden balcony, and near by in a cupboard, a powerful telescope. I spotted their small craft heading out of the bay, careering up and down upon the heavy swell. The children and I crossed on the ferry to Falmouth. and we noticed their small seven foot yacht busily bouncing over the white horses. We shouted from the ferry boat, but the noise of everything, waves, boat engine, wind and seagulls were sufficient to drown our voices. They sped away as we crossed the mouth of the river Fal.

The weather improved over the next few days, and much activity revolved around the tiny harbour. Games were organised for the children once the tide had cleared a patch of sand. When the tide was in, however, the great occupation for the children was fishing off the sea wall. Miles wanted to try his hand at fishing and so I bought a rod and tackle. I so desperately wanted him to catch a fish, and positively prayed that God would reward his efforts. I was reminded that prayer should not be considered as 'twisting' the arm of God, against his will. Miles wanted a fish, and I wanted a new church building for God, and so I decided, sitting watching him with his rod, to put out a 'fleece' before the Lord. To the uninitiated, this simply meant that

I put out a simple test like Gideon, who put out a sheep's fleece in order to get a decision from God. I so desperately needed a direct word from the Lord at St. Mawes and asked God to give me a sign. The sign would be that Miles would catch a fish. Day after day he'd leave the little cottage and make his way down to the quayside. I would make my way around to the far side of the quay, and just outside the shops, I would lean against the stone wall and watch him casting. By the end of the week the rod leaned against the door post forsaken and abandoned, and not a fish in sight!

After two weeks, Celia returned to Tunbridge Wells by train, and I journeyed on with Miles and Kerry. We picked up the caravan and journeyed to Woolacombe, one of the major surfing beaches situated on the north coast of Devon. The pitch we had chosen overlooked the beach and faced west.

The day of our arrival was grey and overcast, there seemed to be no let-up in this rain coming in off the Atlantic. A quick 'recce' of the beach area revealed the tenacious character of the British. With deck chairs and wind-breaks, some people were determined to return to Manchester and Birmingham proving their colour was obtained by sun rather than by rust!

Much to my disappointment we completely overslept, owing to a late card game the previous evening, and missed our Sunday morning worship. The children and I had a small service in the caravan with a Bible reading from Jonah and some prayers. I read from Spurgeon for the day of August 16th . The text was: *'Give unto the Lord the glory due unto his name'* (Psalm 29:2). Within Spurgeon's commentary appear the words:

> It is perhaps one of the hardest struggles of the Christian life to learn this sentence — *'Not unto us, not unto us, but unto thy name be glory'*. It is a lesson which God is ever teaching us, and teaching us sometimes by the most painful of disciplines.

Had I reached a stage in desiring the new building for God, that I was quietly detaching myself and becoming personally burdened, and therefore, in some measure taking too much responsibility upon myself, and thereby taking a glory which was not my own? Before the end of the day, the Lord was to have his way with me.

We spent much of the rest of the day wandering around the shopping centre, looking rather than buying. An enquiry regarding a cash dispenser machine revealed that I would have to make a journey to Ilfracombe. We parked on the quayside, a short walk from the town centre. The little harbour was filled with all sorts of boats, including some luxurious yachts. We walked into town at about 4:30 pm, obtained the money, and the children immediately requested an update on their pocket-money allowance! Armed with three pounds each, Kerry and Miles were determined to spend their money somewhat swiftly. We walked together to a very large putting green. We promised to meet up at 6:30 pm at the church of St. Philip and St. James. Meanwhile I spent some time walking around the gift shops and eventually found a tea-room. It was only half full, and as I felt in a distinctly pensive mood, I wanted to be alone with my thoughts. So I chose a table away from nattering people.

How did I see the way forward? Would we return to the drawing board? Would we frantically hunt the country for money? Should I take a trip to America and raise the cash at some rich church interested in broadcasting the Gospel? I nervously played with the sugar, first making mountains with the grains and then valley's. I found myself entering into the atmosphere of a dull holiday, a dull day, and me in a dull mood. More than ever, I wanted a direct word from God. If anyone had arrived at a decisive moment, it was me. Now the Lord would have to make the situation abundantly clear to me. It was time that the doubts were finally scattered once and for all.

I paid the bill and left for the church. Passing through the line of shops, I made my way up to the putting green to find the children heading towards me eating two very large ice creams. With a quick resumé of the play, and who won what, we made our way to the church.

The church building was grey and austere, a Victorian structure with a clock tower. Below the clock there was a notice which read 'It Is Time To Seek The Lord'. On entering the porch I noticed, from the walls and ceiling, that much repair was long overdue; cracks, peeling paint and mouldy patches were very evident. We made our way down the centre aisle and sat down waiting for the service to start. By the time the vicar stood up to welcome us we were some twenty people in all. The vicar was not robed, simply appearing in a normal grey lounge suit, with a pleasant smile. Beside him sat a lady at an electronic organ consul, announced as 'our guest organist for this evening'. There appeared to be no set pattern to our worship. We sang some familiar pieces. From time to time the vicar would give a text of Scripture, and wanting a word from the Lord I eagerly followed each reference. After some twenty-five minutes a retired gentleman, who had been sitting on the front row, was invited to speak.

'A friendly man', I thought, 'Is he to be my messenger with a word from God?'

As we sat down to hear him, I prayed a most earnest prayer.

'Lord you know how desperately I need your confirmation, or your condemnation, of all that we have done in Your name. We have cried, we have fasted, we have prayed and we have given financially and now, I personally, await your encouragement.'

The preacher (whom I later found out was Ray Pugsley) began with a Bible passage which he proceeded to read himself:

> *'Meanwhile, Saul was still breathing out murderous threats against the Lord's disciples. He went to the high priest and asked him for letters to the synagogues in Damascus, so that if he found any there who belonged to the Way, whether men or women, he might take them as prisoners to Jerusalem. As he neared Damascus on this journey, suddenly a light from heaven flashed around him. He fell to the ground and heard a voice say to him, "Saul, Saul, why do you persecute me?" "Who are you, Lord?" Saul asked. "I am Jesus, whom you are persecuting," he replied. "Now get up and go into the city, and you will be told what you must do".'* (Acts Chapter 9).

I had already guessed the way I thought the sermon was going to go. I imagined he had based Saul's conversion on a clear understanding that there will be someone who had come into church and needed to find Jesus as Lord. He began his address.

'I want to talk to you', he said, 'about God's plan for your life.'

The very word 'plan' was music to my ears.

'God has a unique plan for your life and no other individual has this particular plan because, first, the plan is a personal plan. It is for you alone. It is unique to you. Look at Acts, chapter 9 and verse 6. We read that Saul was specifically told what to do. God had a special task for the Apostle Paul.'

He drew the point out with further illustrations and I responded very positively that God had a plan for my life, but was I at the centre of that plan? The preacher continued.

'I want you to notice further that the plan that God has for your life is a perfect plan, I refer you to Romans chapter 12 and verse 2:

'Do not conform any longer to the pattern of this world, but be transformed by the renewing of your mind. Then you will be able to test and approve what God's will is — his good, pleasing and perfect will.'

For the next ten minutes, this retired gentleman made the point abundantly clear that God has put a lot of time and energy into making the plans for each of our lives faultless. Was I responding to this perfect plan? I felt humanly confident that I had not been grossly disobedient. I wondered what was to follow! The preacher had been speaking for some twenty minutes and he was certainly in full flow as he moved on to another point.

'I would like to close', he went on, 'by telling you that God has a practical plan for your life.'

My mind raced through the Scriptures. Specific instructions to Noah when building the Ark, practical details for Nehemiah when obtaining building materials for the reconstruction of Jerusalem. My heart positively leapt within me. Our plan for the new church will work. It is no 'pipe dream,' it was a vision of God to a man of God for the people of God. Why should I doubt any further?

The evening service came to a close. A lady came over and spoke to me. I began sharing with her the thoughts I had had upon entering the church. Within minutes her husband, plus the vicar (Cyril Tennant), and the preacher all surrounded me. Miles and Kerry stood in the aisle listening to the story of the new church. Ray Pugsley then remarked, 'I have no doubt in my mind that the course upon which God has set you will be accomplished, and that soon.'

These four people around me were led by the vicar to minister to me. Each laid hands upon me and prayed. At that point I began to weep. The time of ministry came to an end and the vicar spoke.

'I have a word for you. It is an unusual word and it may not make much sense, but I offer it to you because I believe the Holy Spirit is prompting me to say the word.'

He shot a glance at the other three people and there was an obvious pause before he spoke.

'The word, I believe, God has for you is 'Christmas'. Does that mean anything to you?'

I said, 'Yes, after more than ten years of agonising and trying to see a vision come to pass, it may very well be that the whole package for the new church will be accomplished this Christmas!'

We left the church and I glanced at my watch. We had been at the service and conversing for the space of two hours. My heart felt lighter and I had truly been ministered to by the Holy Spirit. Outside the church door the preacher tapped me on the shoulder.

'I was tempted, on more than one occasion, to abandon the address given tonight. I now see the reason why God wanted it proclaimed!'

The children and I began our walk back to the car in complete silence. I am sure that they had both entered into the tenderness of the situation and were sufficiently sensitive enough not to raise the subject for fear of embarrassing me. Kerry finally broke the silence.

'Dad,' she began, 'I've *got* to get a present for Emma!'

Soon we were heading back to Woolacombe to finish our holiday.

The next day, Monday, was the best day of our holiday. The sun shone, the beaches were filled, and we had lots of fun surfing. Despite their ages, the children still wanted to surf near me, we jumped the waves together. For the rest of the evening we sat while our ears were bombarded with 104 decibels; the camp was laying on a disco for children. We all went to bed late.

The next few days saw overcast skies and more rain. We returned to 'Littlegarth', Celia's ancestral home. Over breakfast, we talked about planning the day. Betty was always keen that every member of the family know what they are doing. I suggested that we might clean out the swimming pool in the garden. This was thirty-two feet long, eight feet deep, and had a diving board . A couple of years earlier, Celia's sister Venetia had bought her father, Miles, some fish, and he had placed them in the swimming pool. Miles lovingly cared for them, fed them often, and despite the greenness of the pool had an occasional dip at break of day. He had passed away the previous year, and as in all such cases his wife, Betty had needed the familiarity of the fish to remain. But now it was time to remove them. Miles, with the new fishing rod I had bought him at St Mawes, was keen to catch the four trout.

At the evening meal, the subject of the pool came up. Betty wanted the fish disposed of. The children agreed to help and this would mean, as the pool level dropped over the next four days, we would have to take some stiff brushes and scrap away the algae off the sides, and when the level reached three or four inches we would have to wade into thick green slime. After dinner, Miles and I promptly went to the pump house and opened the four inch valve to drain the pool.

Some thirty-six hours later I noticed Miles in the bottom of the pool with Grandad's net, wearing his green Wellington boots. He was pushing the net before him, as the fish scuttled in all directions. Kerry and I were busy hosing down the walls and our level of concentration for the moment, was distracted. Within minutes Kerry climbed down the ladders and stood on the slopping shallow end of the pool. I climbed out and she took hold of the hose. The next minute, with a shriek and a 'clump' Kerry was flat on her back in the green slime. The only thing that was broken was her sense of decorum. After a brief space of laughter and reflection, Miles landed a trout! I grabbed its tail, and clubbed it over the head, as I did with the second, third and fourth. Throughout the rest of that afternoon we saw the last of the green slime disappear down the drainage hole. Later we went in for a well deserved meal. Miles was first to take off his boots before going into the kitchen. He then bellowed, 'Gran, I caught four fish today!'

And God said to me, 'Isn't that what you wanted? — Miles to catch fish?' I felt humbled and deeply gracious to a Father who cared sufficiently to answer my 'fleece'.

Chapter 10

Bring down the fire

Dark clouds were gathering over Rochester as I passed the small airport on the way to see the Bishop. Michael was keen to see me, as it had been some time since we last met. After his 'crunch' letter in August, I wanted to see him. It was now November.

I arrived at Bishopscourt on the stroke of 11:30 am, and was shown into a large living room with cosy comfortable chairs and a coal fire burning in a traditional hearth. The Bishop welcomed me with a hand shake and a warm smile.

'Good to see you, John.'

I was shown a chair by the fire and he sat opposite to me. He then encouraged me to talk about myself, the family and the situation in Tunbridge Wells. I began by saying that we as a fellowship were on a spiritual mountain top. We were seeing some blessing with an increase in numbers and a few people finding Christ for the first time. Our Foundation Course series of Bible studies were being used extensively. Our house groups were having to divide their numbers, a few becoming too large. I spoke for a short while about the family. I told the Bishop that Stephen in his Bible College at Moorlands was a constant source of encouragement. Christopher had just come back from a BBC reporting assignment from Yugoslavia, and the rest of the family were either at school or college. Celia, as always, was a tower of strength and often demonstrated a wisdom beyond her years.

Despite many ups-and-downs, there remained within the congregation a solid core of prayerfully committed people, both to the great commission to spread the Gospel, and God's vision for our future. On the new church front, I felt very excited about the possibilities that lay before us. Having shared the vision with Clive Calver of the Evangelical Alliance, and John Finney (the Archbishop of Canterbury's adviser on the decade of evangelism), our new church offered much scope for broadcasting and televising the Gospel message. We could very well find ourselves recording programmes tailored for any part of the world and linking up with Christian broadcasting stations. Oliver Longley the builder had expressed his desire to build the church, adding: 'Do not change the design, it's a superb building and any changes would ruin the concept'.

Throughout, the Bishop remained silent. I continued talking about the contacts I had made with such people as John Cluny, senior economic analyst to the Independent Television Commission. His letter to me indicated that Television South had lost the battle for the broadcasting licence and this was now going to Meridian. Pat Robertson, a respected Christian evangelist in America was in some way behind Meridian, and so we might obtain a sympathetic connection with Robertson and perhaps some funding from America. The scope for making family television programmes would be enormous in the next few years, with the advent of private companies selling their programmes to the major networks. Tunbridge Wells had plenty of media people and was a natural base for 'know-how.

I continued to emphasise my own interest in broadcasting, and related the times and incidents when I had much to do with local radio and television appearances. I told the Bishop of my involvement with Radio Merseyside and my training at the Television Centre in Bushey. On the ecumenical front I mentioned the School of Evangelism, centred on Christ Church, being inter-denominational with a mixture of lay people and clerics. The use of the radio and television facility in the new church would hopefully be used by other denominations. The ten thousand square feet of recreational space could be made available to the community at large, as the town was totally deficient in this area. During a lull in my personal and parish appraisal, the Bishop thanked me for being open and frank, and remarked that I had spoken for a full half an hour! Now it was his turn, and he pointed out that two themes were uppermost in his mind.

'The first is you John, and the second, is the parish of Christ Church.'

With that opening, he made mention of the high regard in which I was held by many of my colleagues. I was a compassionate man, a loving man and an excellent personal evangelist. Our home was open to all and particularly the poor and needy. He further pointed out that with such gifts and talents, colleagues and friends felt it was difficult for me to enter into a full-orbed ministry, having around my neck, so to speak, the problems of building a new church. Many had spoken to him of my preoccupation with the scheme. Perhaps it was no longer necessary to see the new building in the light of changing circumstances.

'For example,' the Bishop indicated, 'with the rapid changes in radio and television, any church involvement could be at least ten years away, if not more!'

As to his second point, the Bishop intimated that, with the re-ordering of the Parish Boundaries in Tunbridge Wells, this would be the time to phase out the parish altogether, and encourage the congregation to find a new place of worship. This would mean my leaving Tunbridge Wells and finding a parish where I could express all my gifts. He added that this would be no disgrace, as there had been much achieved; and the money from the scheme could be put to other uses. I commented to him that a large proportion of money would go straight to the Church Missionary Society because these funds originally came from a legacy in the form of Crabb Hall, and the will of Miss Crabb stated that either the building be replaced or a percentage of money be given to the society. The remaining £300,000 would be difficult to place — this being the contribution from the congregation. To this his reply was, 'I am relieved to hear this, as I was a little anxious as to what would happen to the money. Perhaps a trust fund could be brought into being and used for the welfare of the parishioners?'

The Bishop paused, either for more thought or with his presentation now complete, and it was at this point that I interjected.

'Bishop, can you honestly see me conducting my ministry in a church in Bradford, for example, knowing full well that I had spent ten years of my life occupied with a scheme that after much expenditure had failed?'

'But John,' he interrupted, 'there are times when we all have to live with failure, and there is no disgrace in that! Indeed, if you were to leave Tunbridge Wells that, in fact, could be to your credit — that you were quite prepared to see the pattern of church ministry changing and you simply moved on to pastures new.'

I could not believe what I was hearing. I decided to tackle things another way.

'Michael,' I said, 'You have just launched a fund to raise one million pounds to establish a Christian Resources Centre for education, training and counselling. You already have your million pounds and your centre is already planned. Could you not see that half-a-million of diocesan investment monies could make this a reality very soon?

This was met with a stony silence. I then quizzed him regarding the money we had already.

'Suppose we go ahead right away and build with the money we have in the bank now?' I challenged.

He twisted in his chair, gazed out of the window and, without looking at me, replied thoughtfully, 'I would not support the creation of a new church in Tunbridge Wells simply as a new centre of worship. There are enough in the town already.'

'Suppose we get the scheme together soon, with all the necessary finance?' I further challenged.

'I would look at it, and weigh up the proposal carefully', he replied with an air of deliberation. He sat up straight.

'I have listened to your agenda John, and you have listened to mine. What we need to do now, is to go away and think about these things, and I shall await a letter from you concerning these matters.'

With that we walked to the front door and shook hands.

I got into my car and reversed out of Bishopscourt Drive, switched on the stereo, and put on my favourite Matt Monroe tape. I began singing at the top of my voice. By now the sun was shining, although the roads remained wet. I was surprised by my reaction to the previous hour-and-a-half. I was not depressed, I was not anxious. I certainly was not over-concerned. Yet I had been informed that it was time that I left my parish to give the Bishop the freedom to close it down. I could only think that the Holy Spirit of God had kept me buoyed at a stage when I could have hit an all-time low. One decision I had to make. Who should know of this day's events? Should the congregation be protected from such a devastating proposal that could likely be initiated by the Bishop, so who would I tell? Celia, was the obvious person, also my faithful friend and Reader, Dick Warren. I had asked some twelve people to pray and if possible to fast for the morning, and these people would need to know the result of our deliberations. Later I was to learn from my eldest son, Stephen, that he and some friends had prayed during Tuesday that God would sustain me, and my meeting with the Bishop would be a positive one. About tea time Sally Sargent had popped in to tell me that earlier in the day, someone had daubed on the walls of the church: 'John Banner — Satanist'. The evil one was getting very agitated It amused me that both the devil and the Bishop were against the scheme. Could it really be possible?

Within a matter of days the 'Four Just Men' were back together planning their strategy. We need to vigorously market the church complex, particularly the commercial element, namely the five shops and the restaurant. Robert agreed to up-date the brochure outlining the planned precinct, and he would further supply new notice boards outside the church, and pursue the Compulsory Purchase Order with the Lands Tribunal. The Tunbridge Wells Borough Council were going to take Crabb Hall by using such powers. John had a meeting planned with Teacher Marks, a forward funding agency to finance the building of the precinct. I would look into the matter regarding American finance through the Robertson Organisation. Parish boundaries were being reordered in the town and a small commission had visited the vicarage to agree the new shape to our district.

November 2nd 1992 was the date fixed for the Deanery Synod. I made my way with some sixty others to Bennett Memorial School. At the top of the Agenda was the subject of the Parish Boundaries within the deanery of the town. There was however, a paragraph in the final report which read as follows:

'We accept that the present plans for the redevelopment of Christ Church represent a major opportunity for Tunbridge Wells. However, if the full proposals cannot be implemented for any reason, we would question the need for another church in the centre of Tunbridge Wells. Within 15 minutes walk of Christ Church there are five existing Anglican churches, we believe that these would be capable of meeting the needs of the residents of the parish of Holy Trinity with Christ Church.'

Somewhere in all this I saw blackmail: 'perform or else'. We had already amalgamated once, Holy Trinity having closed down and the congregation joining Christ Church. Now we were being asked to move for a second time. This I would militantly resist. The thought kept coming to me over and over again: 'Why close down a successful business? We were paying our way in the diocese, winning souls for the kingdom and generally meeting the needs of the community.' Truly water was being poured all over the new church situation. Only days earlier Lesley and I had been sharing the problems confronting Elijah on Carmel, and likened the worsening situation to water being poured on the sacrifice, and then God answering Elijah's prayer, and setting alight the offering and everything with it.

I left the Synod for a 'teach-in' at St.Peter and St.Paul, Tonbridge. This was a series of day seminars on various subjects: today's subject was Worship. The main speaker was Bishop Josiah from Nigeria. It was a beautiful sunny day, but the nearer I got to Tonbridge, the more I became unsettled spiritually. The sessions were well under way, so I crept into the back of a singing seminar. Sitting down, I left a gap between myself and those in the front of the church who were learning how to sing in parts; I was in no mood for praise. Ten years of battling to get a new church and galvanise the congregation was slowly wearing me down. The leader of the singing seminar was a dynamic type, full of music and fun; but I wanted to distance myself from what was happening.

I picked at my fingernails and, looking at my hands, observed the ageing brown liver marks. I well remember, as an apprentice gas fitter, working in sub-zero temperatures on building sites. My young skin would be blue, even mauve with cold, and the back of my hands would burn with pain as the skin dried and cracked.

The singing started with Amazing Grace with four part harmonies. Our teacher was a brilliant girl, Geraldine Latty, whose African roots came out in her joy for the King of Kings. Her white teeth sparkled out of her black face, she was the picture of joy and fulfilment in the Lord.

The afternoon over, Lesley and I made our way to the main church in the town centre. We had a meal and coffee and filed into the evening session. At the chancel steps stood an array of instruments. This had been billed as an African World Night, and

Bishop Josiah would be the preacher. There were many songs to sing and a couple of short dramas. At half-past-nine the Bishop stood up to speak. His text was taken from 1 Kings Chapter 18. I nearly fell off my seat and Lesley just grinned at me.

'Of all the Bible passages to choose, he goes and selects that piece!' I whispered.

The contest on Mount Carmel was a stirring chunk of unadulterated faith. Here was the man Elijah, challenging King Ahab to choose his God. Ahab had chosen his wife's foreign god, Baal instead of the Living God. So the contest takes place on this mountain and 850 of Ahab's false prophets cry to their god all day to send down fire and burn up the bullock for sacrifice. And then comes Elijah's turn. After having a bit of sport with his opponents, he encourages Israel to come near. He then commands twelve barrels of water to be poured over the sacrifice and then asks God to prove himself to Israel by sending down the fire to burn up the offering. Verse 38 reads:

> *'Then the fire of the Lord fell and burned up the sacrifice, the wood, the stones and the soil, and also licked up the water in the trench... When all the people saw this, they fell prostrate and cried, "The Lord he is God! The Lord — he is God!"'*

Two weeks earlier I had freely admitted that the whole episode of everything appearing to be against us was a part of God's overall plan. The 'Four Just Men' were now out of ideas as to how to fund the new church and therefore, if anything was going to happen, then it would have to be God, and God alone, that would bring the whole thing together. I'm sure that God did it so that no glory should be given to another. A miracle we wanted, and only God was in that department.

The days dragged on and I re-read Joshua 1:1-11. Placing myself in the same situation, I stood as Joshua at the entrance of my tent, feeling the pressure of responsibility upon me. How was I going to explain to my half a million people that we were to cross a swollen river Jordan? It was the time of harvest and the river was in flood. How could I ask this nation of Israel to come with me and trust a God who had carried us through so many wilderness experiences? No wonder, when I took over from Moses, God had to encourage me

over and over again. They had trusted Moses, were they going to
trust me the same? I was now challenging them to commit
themselves to me and my judgement!

'Within three days we are to go across this Jordan and enter the
promised land,' I announced.

I was scared stiff of such an ordeal. Did I have the faith for such an
adventure? Was I listening to God, or was I talking to myself? What
would happen if the waters did not part? The people were no doubt
afraid, and had thoughts of the consequences of such an act. Should we,
or should we not, attempt this crossing? I thought about this challenge.

'Lord,' I appealed, 'I am fearful that my faith will fail. How can I
believe when so many are fearful?'

'Have I not commanded you, Joshua, be strong and of a good
courage, I will never leave you nor forsake you'

I felt such a kinship with this man Joshua. I was facing a similar
trial of my faith. Would God act by Christmas as he had promised at
Ilfracombe?

Victor Briggs, a reporter with the *Tunbridge Wells Courier* phoned me a
while later to ask me about the new church scheme.

'Can I pop around and get a story from you?' he enquired.

I was in need of the publicity, so I shared with him the vision that
God had given me. The resultant article appeared on November
27th, and it was superbly written. I recall saying to someone in the
congregation the following Sunday: 'Now, I have put my foot in it!'

Yes, my feet were in the water, and now we waited for the waters
to divide. John Kain had for some time desired an attractive brochure
to put before clients interested in the scheme, especially on the
investment side. So Pym, Val and I set to and worked our way through
a sixteen page presentation booklet. Within days, Pym was rushed into
hospital with problems with her heart pace-maker. Shortly after that
Val was visiting specialists in London for glaucoma. I reflected on these
things. Everyone associated with this project was now subject to some
sort of major challenge. A few days later I was put out of action with a
high temperature — it appeared that the devil was working overtime!
But for all his efforts he had no hope of winning, we were all clinging
too tightly to God. That hold on God was now to be tested to the limit.

December 19th was a typical Saturday morning. The hoover was whirring, the washing machine was particularly noisy and I was faced with a pile of Christmas cards to open. I escaped to the quietness of my study, and ignoring most of the obvious seasonal cards, began opening the A4 white envelopes. The third letter was from the Bishop. It began by mentioning the newspaper article of November 27th, in which I had said to a journalist that I was confident that the new year would bring some encouragement. The Bishop went on to write concerning my lack of correspondence, albeit the two months that we agreed upon for my formal reply to his proposal to leave the diocese, had not expired. He continued on about the scheme, mentioning that revised plans were unacceptable to him as we would only be building a new church. My immediate reaction to this was 'What new plans?' None had been drawn up to my knowledge, though there had been talk in the PCC to reduce the cost of the proposed building by making substantial savings. The penultimate paragraph contained the words, 'I shall therefore be recommending to the Diocesan Pastoral Committee that the scheme for Christ Church, now lodged with the Church Commissioners, be withdrawn.'

The Bishop had once again been goaded into action by the arch-enemy of the plans — the devil, and he using Deanery Synod people to do his work! For a Bishop to write such a thing to any of his clergy immediately before Christmas was totally unacceptable. He had wrecked my summer holiday with a similar tactic, and now it was a repeat showing. This time however, things were hotting up. While devastated by the letter, I nevertheless thought that Satan was finally having his last fling, and of all people, to use my Bishop. The man who eighteen months earlier had said publicly to the congregation, 'You and your project has my full and personal whole hearted support,' was now reneging and becoming a militant opponent of the scheme.

With a heavy heart I rang John, Robert and Dick. Each made his own particular comment, but the surprising outcome resulted in none of us taking the Bishop seriously. We had come a long way in prayer, in fasting and jolly hard work, and none of us could see that all this could come to an abrupt end by the remarks of one man.

I phoned Lesley later in the day. She, full of faith and confidence, brushed aside the Bishop's letter and, more than ever, she could see that this was all part of the divine strategy. Celia's remarks that we would win through whatever the challenge came as a great encouragement to me.

Another event later on the 19th was to put things in proportion and to make me realise that people mattered more than things. Two days earlier, a gentleman had rung Celia. The subject of the conversation was simply that the man was desperately confused, felt at times disoriented; and was seeking urgent spiritual help. Seeing the scribbled note on my desk to ring him, I spoke to him and invited him to the vicarage in the late afternoon. Stephen was a tall man, some six-foot-two in height. Sitting in my study I found myself saying that his present condition could very well be prompted by the Holy Spirit, and he should not be over-troubled by the various spiritual vibrations that were now prompting him to seek Christian counsel. I learned that he taught Religious Knowledge in one of the local schools. My inner spirit leapt for joy, for to win such a man for Christ would be a triumph of God's grace! I carefully and gently presented the good news of Christ to him. He listened with a marked degree of intensity, almost hanging on my every word. Then I came to the question, 'Does this make sense to you?'

'Yes', he replied.

Our occupations brought a degree of 'eye-ball to eye-ball' contact, and I could detect not so much desperation, but a hungering and a thirsting after righteousness. Something inside me felt deeply concerned for this lonely man.

'Would you like to receive Jesus Christ as your Saviour and Lord?'

Again his reply was in the affirmative. I quietly instructed him as to my intentions in leading him into a right relationship with God. I would pray a prayer introducing him to God, and God to him. The second prayer would be for him to follow, phrase by phrase, a simple acceptance of Jesus Christ. For a final prayer, I would stand and lay my hand upon him to receive the Holy Spirit, confirming his new found faith. We passed through each of these prayer phases and as I laid my hand upon his head, I believe God whispered to me, 'This is the real work of the Kingdom.'

I further mused at a £2 million building in exchange for a soul. There was no comparison. One person won to Christ was far more priceless than any earthly man-made object, and I would freely sacrifice the same to win anyone to the Lord.

After a brief conversation we shook hands, and I said to him, 'Welcome to the family of God!'

The faintest twitch of his face had within it the birth of a smile. He picked up his bags in the hall and left with a polite 'thank you.' I returned to the study and felt a tear straining to be released, the emotion of the day was now getting through to me. From the slough of despondency and the cold hand of despair, within a few hours I was taken into the heavenlies, with all the rapturous joy of knowing that another soul was saved for eternity.

By December 20th, all the children were home. It had been a considerable time since we had all been together. Last Christmas, Nicola had been in Australia and hence we were incomplete, but now our numbers had swollen to twelve as we entertained three members of our congregation and a student from Nicola's agriculture college.

While the festivities were lighthearted, nevertheless I could not get the Bishop's letter out of my mind. It acted as a continuous blight throughout the Christmas period. A welcome change of pace found me giving out Christmas parcels in the parish, complete with new ten pound notes. Four or five families I knew of were finding life very difficult and my appearance, three days before Christmas standing on the doorstep, was a bit like the visit of Father Christmas. At one point in my rounds, I was ably assisted by two scruffy fourteen-year-old boys. One of them possessed a wisdom beyond his years, and told me of a very needy family. I found myself on the doorstep.

'We don't need any Christmas hampers from anybody. There are more people in need than us. Perhaps you can go to another house?'

With that the lady duly sent me on my way! But as she did so, she stepped forward to close the door and made a comment to one of the fourteen year olds. 'Ben, don't you be later than nine-thirty!'

Would you believe it, this 'Artful Dodger' had led me to his own front door!

Requiring a breath of fresh air, I parked the car in the vicarage and walked round to Madeira Park and a nursing home. I glanced up at Lillian's bed-sit window. The light was still on so I gently knocked on the door. Within minutes I was sitting with her. You will recall that

Lillian and Fergie had been together supporting the work of the Rwanda Mission, sending parcels to Africa in such a Victorian fashion that even the missionaries were amused to find Marmite wrapped into sheets that would eventually be turned into bandages. Fergie had died a year earlier, and now Lillian, well into her nineties, lived in a delightful little room overlooking the wooded area of Warwick Park. The days of her capture by the Nazi's, and her exile from her beloved Channel Islands to France, were now a piece of history. On the little table next to her bed, were the current batch of letters still going to the 'children' she had once taught on the Island of Guernsey.

'And how is the new church going?' she enquired. 'I pray for you and the congregation every day.'

I began to state all the happenings since the summer. While I was sharing the events I began to feel a large lump in my throat, the more I continued the more break-up in my voice appeared. By the time I had spoken about the Bishop's last letter I felt the tears running down my face. She remained silent and just looked with immense compassion as I struggled with the tale. I stopped in mid-sentence and completely broke down. With my head in my hands I wept bitterly. She kept repeating: 'Oh!, Mr. Banner, dear Mr. Banner,' and then she said, 'Oh! Dear God'.

I struggled with a handkerchief and at least felt some relief in having blown all the tension and all the disappointment into the lap of a lady who had known much pain and hardship. There hung in the air a silence, lasting a good three minutes. I had nothing more to say, and she agonised with me. The clock beside her bed ticked incessantly. The occasional car passed down the road. The dimly lit room seemed to be as if we were both neither in the light nor in the dark, but rather in a twilight of sorts. Lillian spoke first.

'Mr. Banner, build the church first, I believe that's what God wants.'

I reassured her that God would build this church, and even the gates of hell would not stop it.

'Can we pray?' she asked.

I nodded an agreement. Holding each others hands, we gave God the problem. I could not pray and was content to leave Lillian's prayer with a simple 'Amen'. I got up to leave and bent over and kissed her forehead. 'God loves you. And so do I', I said, and with that I left.

Out in the brisk fresh air, I reflected upon the therapeutic time that I had just obtained. Time with Lillian seemed to fly by and underneath the street lamp, I checked my watch. It was eleven-thirty. I looked up at her bedroom window, the bedside light was still on and somehow I knew she was continuing to pray. Over Christmas I had learned from congregational members that a number of them had written to the Bishop in support of having our new church. This was a great encouragement. The evil one, however, had not completed his works and shortly after Christmas, I learned, painfully, that some former members of the congregation had been casting aspersions upon my character, which ultimately upset Celia and the family. It was seen as yet another attack from the evil one. Deeply hurt, I wrote to the Bishop.

Three days later, he rang me half way through a meal. I took the call in the study, away from the family.

'Bishop Michael here, John. I have just read your letter and, I am saddened that you have been hurt in this way. I want you to know that you have my full support and prayers, and, after all that you have gone through, to have this as well, must be truly hurtful for you and Celia.'

His words touched a very tender spot, here was my Bishop sharing this agony with me and deeply empathising in my situation.

'Michael, thank you for phoning me. I am grateful for your support and encouragement. It has been a difficult Christmas, but I do believe that the devil has shot his last bolt! I believe that we have to go forward with faith and encouragement that God will work his purposes out as he so wishes. I am saddened by the fact that the evil one can use Christian people for his own purposes.'

The Bishop continued with a very compassionate and tender tone to his voice — my respect for him was growing by the minute.

'John,' he continued, 'I suggest I meet with you and the PCC on February 10th, if that's convenient. Then let us have a spiritual time of sharing, of finding a common mind, and moving together concerning the new church. Let us pray concerning the meeting, and let us not come to any rapid conclusions, but determine God's will for the future together.'

I agreed that this was the best way forward, and we bade each other every good wish and blessing for the New Year. I replaced the phone and reflected upon the scheduled meeting. The PCC, with the Bishop, would make a decision the day before the Pastoral Committee meeting. This clearly gave us no time for reflection, prayerful consideration, and ultimately the right decision. We would, therefore, have to start praying now! It would be a meeting of 'minds', with mutual respect for the way God had brought us, and where he was leading us.

I left the study and walked into the kitchen. Celia had finished her meal and there was a distinct look of expectancy upon her face.

'Well?' she asked. 'What did the Bishop want?'

I shared our conversation with her and, as we sat together at the table holding hands, we prayed and thanked God that he was continuing to show us his love and compassion in the most difficult of climates. We both, discretely, wiped a tear away and got on with the job of living.

Chapter 11

Washed out in Eastbourne

By January 4th I was feeling thoroughly washed out, mentally tired, and physically unfit. I shared the pressures with Celia, and by Tuesday lunch-hour, I had packed a few things and driven down to Eastbourne. Most of the better quality hotels were situated on the sea front. Having left home in a torrential downpour, I had rather expected the weather to clear up, but it was not to be. I stayed at the Cumberland Hotel. My room was situated on the first floor. It was warm, bright, and very comfortable, with a nice en-suite bathroom. I took off my wet coat and hung it outside the wardrobe to dry. Kicking off my shoes, I removed my jacket, and stood at the bottom of the bed and fell backwards onto it with a sigh. I lay there for a few minutes, wondering why I was there. Why had I made the effort? Was it to get the church and its problems out of my system? Was it to run away from home, which was also my place of work? Something which had always bugged my system? Or was I trying to run away from myself?

At 4:30 pm I rang Celia. The phone was engaged, so I spent some time unpacking my case. The rain was now audibly firing its pellets upon the window pane and, distracted by it, I went over to the main window, overlooking the sea. Pushing my nose against the window pane, I was confident that the elements could not, and would not, touch me now! I was fully insulated from the ravages of the storm in more ways than one. Thirty yards away, the sea was pounding and crashing on the promenade, sending its spray sprawling across the coast road. It was growing dark. The occasional car passed beneath the hotel, its bright lights an immediate contrast with the encircling gloom. My mind went back to the Bishop's letter of December 19th. Still with my nose against the window pane, my tears began to flow. I turned round and sat down at the desk with the hotel note paper in front of me, and I wept uncontrollably for a full two minutes.

My mind flashed back to the hundreds of meetings that I had had with town planners, architects, consulting engineers, Church commissioners and the like. Had I wasted these thousands of hours, and tons of papers, all to no avail? Had I spent the finest ten years of my life on a wasted cause? Had I wasted time, money, and led my congregation up a blind alley? In short, was I a failure? Could I face admitting this to Celia, the family, and to my congregation? After this who would have me in another parish? Where could I go? What other job could I do?

I suddenly realised that I was doing the devil's work for him. I was becoming negative, entering into a slough of despondency, and the huge word 'doubt' was beginning to pervade all my thinking. A number of texts running like a computerised message along a conveyor belt appeared in the back of my mind:

'I can do all things through Christ who strengthens me.'

'I will fulfil all your plans.'

'If God be for us, who can be against us?'

'Let us rebuild the wall of Jerusalem and rid ourselves of this disgrace.'

I began now to feel that the Word of God was like a soothing 'balm of Gilead', and I was being relieved from the pain of the moment. The note paper had become soggy with my tears. I made a conscious decision to have a bath, and tried to forget all but the texts which had been such a comfort to me. I would then ring Celia. Within a matter of minutes, I lay in the bath and, glancing up at the window, I noticed that it was now completely dark.

A further half-an-hour went by. I made my way down to the reception to check the time of the evening meal, and was told that dinner was now being served. Tables were laid, and seating arranged for about one hundred people. I smiled as the head waiter conducted me to a table upon which stood a plaque with my room number on it. I mused, even in winter, the system goes on!

Soon the wine waiter came over and I ordered a half bottle of their house red. Within a matter of minutes a middle aged couple with very strong Yorkshire accents sat behind me. It was quite clear, from their conversation, that they were enjoying a winter break. I overheard her say, 'Len it's a luvely 'otel.'

'Eee and it's a riiight good priiice too,' he responded.

'Shull we 'ave stake?' she murmured, as if it was not her usual fare. He was much more inclined to take the fish on the menu, which was caught locally. The waiter came over to take their order. He spoke with a French accent and made the couple feel entirely at home, and suggested various extra vegetables that would delight the pallet. Len, however, was keeping to his usual diet and he was not going to be swayed by *choux-au-gratin*, and when asked if 'Monsieur would like *pommes-frites*', he replied that 'Chips would do very niiicely, thank thee'.

The meal finished, I walked back to reception to enquire about the night life, and was told that there was a board on which was featured all the local theatres, cinemas, and places of exhibition. Perusing through the handouts, I noticed one entitled: The Eastbourne Hippodrome, featuring, 'The Sound of Music'. The starting time was 7:30 pm. I had got just ten minutes to get there!

Outside the rain was continuing to lash down, and I desperately tried to find someone who would tell me the whereabouts of the Hippodrome. Within minutes I was in a quaint little theatre, positively enthralled by the building itself. There were tiny boxes, hanging on each side of the stage, a balcony, which at the present time was not overcrowded, and the usual orchestral pit. The orchestra was truly ad hoc. To the right, playing trombone, was a man who, every now and again, would encourage a young teenager, possibly his son, who was one of two trumpeters for the night. To the left, there was a man, seated on a high stool, with a very large double bass. On his left was the drummer. In front of them both sat the pianist, but as yet, there was no conductor. In front of the trumpeters were two girl violinists. In front of them was another girl, playing instruments from oboe to clarinet. An overture was struck up, and the lady at the piano also became the conductor. All the familiar phrases from The Sound of Music could be picked out, as this little orchestra began what was to be an extremely delightful and well-spent two hours with Maria, the Captain, and his charming children. After two encores, the assembled cast waved from the stage, and the curtain fell. It was with some disappointment that the atmosphere of light, colour, sound and activity, all suddenly stopped. For two hours I had been in the Austrian Tyrol, surrounded by the music, the personalities of the people. I had been totally lost in the delight of it all.

Stepping outside into the dark street and the wet of the night, my mind went back to 1944. My father had left me in a cinema, aged eight, and I had been watching a film with Fred Astaire and Ginger Rogers. Massive screen sets with hundreds of dancing girls accompanied by men in tall toppers. At the centre of the cascading staircase had been these two stars, that seemed to hold all the happiness that so many of us wanted in the drab wartime England of 1944.

Back at the hotel I sat down in the very large, plush lounge. Apart from two octogenarian ladies, sitting quite separately, one with her head buried in a book, the other writing on a pad on her knee, the lounge was empty. Within twenty minutes, I returned to my room and phoned home. I spoke to Stephen, asked him to pass on the message to Mum that I was well settled in at the Cumberland Hotel, and would be home some time on Thursday.

On Wednesday I scurried down to breakfast. It was still raining. Outside the passing cars made a shsssss noise as they sped along the flooded sea front. The occasional True Brit defied the torrential rain and could be seen taking a constitutional. By lunch hour I had walked the whole of the sea front. Realising that early January was still the season of pantomimes, I noticed a billboard advertising Dora Brian appearing in 'Cinderella'. After the evening meal I joined the audience shouting the familiar, 'Yes he will... No he won't... Yes he will!!' at the pantomime. Dora was superb. The show finished at about 10:15 pm.

Within a matter of minutes I found myself in a little bar and, after ordering a coffee, I sat near to two gentlemen, both drinking Guinness. My thoughts wondered. I had heard from one or two objectors to our scheme that there were too many churches in Tunbridge Wells. So, I asked myself a question, 'How many churches are there in Eastbourne?' My two 'Guinness' gentleman informed me: 'Ten or twelve I suppose, in the immediate town centre.'

I then briefly told them who I was, and why I was asking the question. Bernard, the Irishman's pal, made a significant reply concerning the Tunbridge Wells congregation: 'You're a living body of people, you have raised the money yourselves, and you have a divine right to build a church for your congregation'.

With that and thanks to them both I left saying, 'You have given me much courage, goodnight and God bless'.

By the time I got back to my hotel room I was soaked through to the skin and promptly had a hot shower, and strung up my coat and trousers to dry. After breakfast the following morning, I checked out and journeyed home.

At the vicarage, Stephen was pouring over a map of the world. He was into his missiology year at his Bible college, and having spent some time writing up on missions was, for this penultimate term, going to Peru for ten weeks with the organisation Latin Link. A few days before he was due to leave, he asked me about a last will and testament. I told him, 'You could make a will on the back of sweet paper, as long as it is signed and witnessed.' He wrote his final testament, placed it in an envelope and put it away.

News from Peru was not good. *World Prayer News*, a missionary publication issued in the previous December had reported: 'During a sharp upsurge of terrorist violence in Lima in late July, Sendero's leaders claimed publicly that they would occupy the Presidential Palace by February 1993. The head of the Sendero Luminoso terrorist group had been captured by the Peruvian anti-terrorist squad at the beginning of September, along with other senior organisation members. It would be foolish to assume that this will bring about an immediate end to the violence, but pray that Sendero supporters will become disillusioned as the leaders are brought to trial. Money is being solicited in European capitals, including London for the support of this brutal and inhuman movement.'

On Wednesday January 13th 1993, we stood in the drive of our house with the car packed. It included a bag that Stephen had picked up from Latin Link headquarters in London, containing letters, clothes, medical goods and some luxuries for Latin Link missionaries. Having said an emotional good-bye to Celia, Stephen and I drove to Gatwick airport. Conversation for the first time was difficult. During one of these silences, I was painfully aware that this may be the last day I would see my son and the feeling got steadily worse as we approached the airport. After processing the ticket and baggage, we went for a coffee. Again I felt the atmosphere thick with apprehension. I kept reminding myself, 'He is God's own. God will look after him.'

Stephen's flight number came up, and we made our way to the departure area.

'Well Dad, I must go.'

He threw his arms around me and I held him tight.

'Go for it son, the Lord is with you,' I said.

I watched him as he went through passport control, showed his documents and before the X-ray machine he turned back, gave a quick wave, and was out of sight. I walked back through the booking hall with a large lump in my throat I journeyed back to Tunbridge Wells idling at some 35 mph.

On Monday 25th January, Graham Reed rang from his office in London to inform me that he had met representatives from Kent Skill, a local arm of the Enterprise Board. If unemployed people could be occupied on our building programme, it could save us up to £300,000. Over the phone this sounded extremely exciting and could make the difference between 'make or break' regarding the finances of the new church.

Within a couple of weeks, two of the Kent Skill managers came to the vicarage and spoke about their organisation and what it could achieve. Since receiving the contract prices in April 1992, all of us on the team had worked very hard to make some severe reductions in the cost of the building. The lowest estimate came from Longley's at some £2.5 million. By now it was quite clear that informal talks with the Managing Director, Oliver Longley, and his team, should continue.

The meeting that the Bishop wished to hold with me and the PCC took place on February 10th. He opened the meeting by saying that he was under pressure from the Church Commissioners, and dates previously set for some activity on site had as yet not been met. Peter Law asked regarding the financial aspect and Robert and John stressed the problem as a 'chicken and egg' situation. Signing up tenants for a non-existent precinct was clearly not the way forward, however forward funding was required in order to make the commercial aspect of the scheme financially viable. I had written a lengthy report to the Bishop clearly pointing out the need for the building with regard to the community. He closed the meeting by reaffirming his belief that the church should be 'in the market place'. It was agreed that we meet in four months time. The upshot of the meeting was that we were all under episcopal pressure to perform, and the Bishop would not tolerate any further procrastination. It was now imperative to meet the favoured contractor James Longley, and pursue the savings that could be made with Kent Skill. And so we met together in the church hall on the morning of the February 25th 1993. After a two hour meeting and buffet lunch, we said our goodbyes. On shaking hands, Oliver Longley said to me, 'It's a beautiful scheme and worthy of success, I would love to build it.'

The rapport which we had established with Longley's was a sure sign that they were becoming the favourite contractor to build the new church.

Chapter 12
The sands of time

Our daughter Nicola had been out in Australia. Now she had returned to the UK and it was becoming abundantly clear that she wished to stay home and pursue a career in agriculture.

By March 19th we were looking forward to seeing Stephen back from his hair-raising South American tour. Indeed, he confessed that while in Peru, the sound of gunfire appeared to get closer to the village in which he was ministering with the local pastor.

Meanwhile, back at the ranch, Celia was reaching her fiftieth birthday and that called for some sort of celebration. The children and I were anxious to see that Celia had a party to remember. So, in the days that followed, I walked up to the Calverley Hotel and spoke to the owners. We planned a superb meal with a nice long polished table complete with silver and candles, and every effort was made to keep this a surprise.

By 6 pm on her birthday the children, by a pre-arranged plan, were making all their own arrangements to go out for the evening. They left the vicarage wishing Celia and I a pleasant evening's meal together! Indeed, two members of the family had gone out in their scruffy jeans and were going to change their clothes a little later. About 7 pm, Celia and I set off and toured the town on the pretence that I was looking for an appropriate place to have a meal. I pulled into the Calverley Hotel car park, much to Celia's surprise.

'This is a bit up market isn't it?' she exclaimed.

'It's a special occasion. It's your birthday,' I said, not making any effort to remind her this was her fiftieth.

Upon entering the hotel reception area we made our way through to the bar. Celia was confronted by our six children, all sitting around two bar tables complete with drinks. It was quite obvious that Celia had no idea that we would celebrate her birthday together. Within half-an-hour we entered the restaurant and the staff had prepared a table beautifully laid-out with flowers and a celebration bottle of champagne at the ready. Some way through the meal Nicola, the born comedienne of the family, asked a young waitress for a glass of water. Ten minutes later it failed to arrive. She asked another girl, but again failure to deliver followed. Finally, in desperation, and with the family in heaps of laughter, she removed the flowers from the middle of the table and filled her glass with water from the vase! Adding to our excitement, we talked about the planned trip to Les Arc skiing resort in the French Alps, arranged by Celia some couple of months earlier. On March 27th we flew out of Gatwick airport for Lyon, followed by a three hour coach journey into the Alps.

Les Arc 2000 is about 2000 metres above sea level, and therefore well into the snow line and providing skiing well into April. Our hotel accommodation was in a six-storey building and as there were eight of us we took two rooms opposite one another across the corridor. The four boys were in the same room facing Mont Blanc to the north. Celia and I, and the girls, faced the ski slopes. As I stood on the veranda the following morning observing the early skiers, I reflected that most of the excitement of my life seemed to occur in later years. At age forty-six I took a balloon flight from Tunbridge Wells to the Boars Head, some six miles away, complete with cassock and old fashioned flying helmet. At fifty, I decided to do a sponsored parachute jump, in aid of the new church funds, so my son Stephen, plus three friends, including the local undertaker's son, spent a weekend at Headcorn airfield. And here I was, skiing for the first time at fifty-six... I must be mad!

With borrowed ski-jacket and salopettes, hired boots and skis, all eight of us went down to the first ski lift, and so began a very happy holiday. Two incidents are rivetted in my memory. On the second day Stephen decided to take a Blue run, which was slightly more difficult than the norm. To get to the ski lift, he and I approached a vicious forty-five degree slope down, and perching ourselves on top I suddenly realised that this was not snow, it was sheer ice. I shouted to

Stephen, 'I'd sooner do another parachute jump than go down that!'

He asked me to 'plough', which means bringing the front of both skis together to a point. I attempted this and promptly fell over.

'Right, we'll try this,' he said. He faced down the slope with his skis in a plough position and asked me to lock my skis into his, standing right behind him.

'Grab me round the waist Dad, tight, and when I say *Go* open your skies parallel.'

The slope was some two kilometres long with a wooded area at the bottom, and some people standing idly around. I then heard Stephen shout, 'Geronimo!'. We both opened our skis, and I honestly felt we must have touched some sixty or seventy miles an hour. All I could see was that we were heading for the wood, and startled people were watching our idiotic antics! I was quite convinced the end of my life had arrived.

'How do I pronounce the last rights upon myself?' I wondered. Pictures of people with legs astride a tree crossed my mind. Stephen then shouted, 'Turn left!' My skis, inside his, just followed suit and we skidded to a halt. I promptly sat in the snow and said, 'Don't ever ask me to do anything like that again!' But within minutes even worse was to happen!

We shuffled our skis to the ski lift, and instead of chairs to take us to the top of the mountain, there were poles. Stephen politely asked me to go in front of him. Unfortunately I had not been watching the person in front of me, who was half way up the mountain before I realised that it was my turn and I didn't know what to do. The two attendants were in full conversation and not interested in what was happening at the start of the lift. I shuffled my skis through the narrow, horizontal poles at waist height, the ski sticks were in my right hand. The pole that was to take me up the hill was some seven feet long, with a sort-of nine inch plate at the bottom upon which I presumed I was supposed to sit. Grabbing the pole in my left hand, I sat down on the plate which, to my surprise, went straight to the ground. Little did I know that the action of pulling on the pole connected it to the cable and while I was beginning to stand up and compose myself, I was promptly dragged up the mountain. My grip on the pole was sliding down to the plate. A short glance back to the attendants, found them standing with horrified looks as I was now being dragged at full stretch, and unable to use my right hand to enhance my hold. I again looked back in sheer helplessness to see Stephen crippled up in laughter.

The ski lift finally coincided with a horizontal stretch and I was able to grab the pole higher up and put the plate in between my legs. The grooves in the snow for the skis were quite obvious and so I put my skis in the pathway. I now, for the first time, felt at some ease. However, to my shock and surprise, the ski lift then coincided with a slope down and not up, and I discovered that I was now going faster than the lift and all my composure was now wrecked in one foul swoop. I shouted back to Stephen, 'Give me a parachute jump any day!'

The ski lift now coincided with a forty-five degree slope upwards and by now there was little strength in my left hand to grip. At that moment one ski came out of its groove and locked across the other ski, and so I ploughed into some soft snow and fell over to my left. I was relieved to be off the lift and reclining with some ease, when I noticed that Stephen behind me was approaching rather quickly, and I now had to get out of the way. A glance up the hill revealed that I was some twenty meters from the top. Stephen arrived, and in great peals of laughter we went to another ski lift and this time, much to my great relief, it was of the 'chair' variety.

One further incident involved Celia. The three girls were on a chair lift, Mum, Kerry and Nicola. Three of the boys had arrived at the top of the slope, with Stephen and I following behind. When her chair arrived at the summit carousel the three girls were pelted with snow balls by Christopher, Russell and Miles. Nicola and Kerry jumped off the chair, being the right thing to do, but unfortunately Celia was distracted and to her horror she found herself going round the carousel and heading back down the mountain. She threw herself off the chair and landed unceremoniously in a pile of snow. The look on her face was one of horror, anger and total bewilderment. Needless to say the children came in for some sharp tongued advice!

Each evening, after dinner, one of the boys led us in a 'thought for the day', reading a passage from the Bible and then commenting upon it. All of us prayed individually, just a short prayer, and I know that Celia and I became very emotional at this very lovely event of all of our children expressing their love for the Lord, and the way in which we were gelling as a family. Russell in particular, in picking his subject and his mode of delivery, had all the hallmarks of a natural pastor.

Home again, and with life back to normal, I had a telephone call from Robert Wickham. He persuaded me that he was quite correct in urging us to get the costs of the new building down to £1.9 million. Considerable savings would have to be made, and this was a matter we would have to take up with the architect. Over the weeks ahead I was in much prayer that God would give us the wisdom to make the right decisions, and if we needed to make savings, this would clearly effect the overall look of the development.

On Friday April 16th I rang John Kain.

'John,' I said, 'I believe that the time has come for a whole new look at the way forward for the new church. I would like to put a proposal to Brenda and Graham, and I suggest that we give them a ring and see them next Monday.'

'What's on your mind?' he replied

'A Phased Scheme. That would be a real possibility!' I conjectured.

Monday arrived, and by 10:30 we were in the architects office.

'In view of the failure of Gladdings Secured Contracts, our partner in the Scheme,' I began, 'I would like to suggest that we put before the Diocesan Board of Finance a proposal to build the church in 3 phases. Phase 1 would build the car park and church with the church hall as a shell. Phase 2 would be to build the shops when the property market came back into prominence and was seen as a sound investment. Phase 3 will kit out comprehensively the Worship Centre and the Parish Hall.'

A general discussion followed. The sun was now shining upon the polished table and almost gave a calming effect despite the raised voices. For some time we banded about our ideas and how savings could be made to get the cost of Phase 1 down to a reasonable level. From Graham's assessment of the financial outlay to build the Car Park and Worship Centre above, with limited utilities, this could serve us well for a couple of years. After that it was felt that the property market would pick up, and the precinct could then be built as Phase 2, providing five shops and a restaurant in the High Street, at a building cost, of say, £350,000 and having a market value of

£1 million. The profit on the precinct could now provide the furnishings and fittings to the church and the church hall with associated offices.

For our part, we were still agonising about the pattern of phasing and in particular, the costs involved. From what Graham was saying, Phase 1 would cost some £1.3 million. With the settlement of a Compulsory Purchase Order we would reach this figure, and therefore we were quite confident that the Diocese would accept this proposal.

'After all, no church building in Great Britain had ever been built with all the money up front to begin with!' I commented.

We were now on our own, I thought, and would we be able to prove to the Bishop and Church Authorities that the contract could go ahead on the basis of the Phasing we had planned. And, while I was full of optimism, it was quite clear to me that within the Church of England's ranks there were some very hard headed business types who would like to see the money before spending it.

At home I was welcomed by Celia: 'How did it go today?'

'I'm confident that we can phase the scheme, but my problem will be putting all this in a comprehensive way to influence the doubters on the Diocesan Board of Finance.'

'Well darling,' she replied, 'God has brought us this far, I can't see him abandoning us now. We must believe that he is on our side and seeing his own will and purpose fulfilled.'

In order to bring members of the Diocesan Board of Finance up to date, and to give them historical background information and the present thinking on the phased scheme, Lesley, my church warden, assisted me in drawing up a brochure which we called, 'Pathways to Progress.' Within a matter of days, I personally delivered the brochures to various members of the DBF, lobbying them at the same time to give us the 'go-ahead' and to approve the financial package.

The following Sunday I preached on 'Where is the God of Elijah?' This sermon was part of a character study I was doing on this favourite prophet of mine. I was beginning to feel something of the challenge of the moment, as well as the loneliness of my situation, like Jack Cornwall in the Battle of Jutland standing alone by his gun in a most difficult hour.

Within two weeks of our meeting in London, the entire design team, plus Longley's management, met at the latter's headquarters in Crawley in an attempt to effect more savings. We were twelve in number, and a good deal of the time was spent on attempting to make a saving on what appeared to be a very complicated roof design, drawn up by our structural engineer. Longley's agreed to consult with a roof firm and, if possible, come up with a cheaper alternative. One aspect of the structure included a circular stainless steel beam at the base of the steeple. Despite my protestations from the early days that modern steeples in light weight materials always suffered whip-lash, and hence were prone to leakage, nevertheless the architect had incorporated into the design a steeple. We all agreed that time was required to make these emendations, but unfortunately the Diocese and the Bishop were pressing for a final solution. I reminded the assembled group that we had three weeks only to effect changes as our scheme had to come before the Diocesan Board of Finance on June 15th.

Journeying back with John Kain and Dick Warren we stopped for a coffee at a country pub, and reflected upon the five hours with the Longley Management team. Considerable savings were being made, not least a whole re-design of the roof. The stainless steel girders in the steeple would be replaced with cheaper material, and it was estimated that some saving of £130,000 could be made.

At home I opened my mail to see a letter written by the Rural Dean dated 31st May, on behalf of the Standing Committee of the Deanery Synod (the local parliament for some twenty churches with representatives from each church, including the vicars). The letter was a copy that had been sent to the Bishop in which it stated that it was the view of the Deanery Synod that a new church in the High Street was no longer required, and any rebuilding should be opposed. I was horrified that half a dozen people, including the Deanery Synod Lay Chairman, who militantly opposed the scheme, had taken it upon themselves to speak for the Synod, a body numbering some eighty to ninety people. I promptly wrote back to Bob (the Rural Dean) and asked what mandate he had received from the full synod to write such a letter to the Bishop. Two committee members of the synod that I contacted by phone had no knowledge of the letter sent to the Bishop, as they had been absent at the last standing committee meeting.

The next scheduled date for the full synod to meet was June 12th. This was a Saturday morning gathering in the lovely church of Lamberhurst in Kent, some four miles from Tunbridge Wells. It was a lovely day and I chose to drive alone. Within half a mile of my vicarage I was virtually out in the open country, so I decided to set out early and drive slowly.

I parked the car and spoke to Clive Porthouse, the vicar of Southborough. I shared with him the contents of the letter from Bob Whyte. Clive looked at the sky in sheer disbelief and frustration and simply said, 'John it gets tougher by the minute. You get in there and tear a strip off them!'

Inside the church it was cool and, for a change, quite crowded. I chose a dark, pitch pine pew at the rear of the church. I decided I would raise the matter of the letter under 'Any Other Business.' One item on the Agenda was a vacancy for a clergyman on the Standing Committee, and so I put my name forward and was elected! My determination to keep the Standing Committee on the straight and narrow, after this debacle, was strong and determined. The meeting took about an hour and a half, and the penultimate item on the Agenda was Any Other Business. The Rural Dean spoke: 'As there are no matters under Any Other Business, I declare...'

At that moment I stood up.

'May I ask the Rural Dean what authority the Standing Committee had in sending this letter to the Bishop? And for members who are not aware of the contents of the letter, I shall take the trouble to read it.'

I stood up and read slowly and with some determination. The first person to speak up was the former Rural Dean, Jeffrey Hyder. In a nutshell, he questioned the authority of the Standing Committee to write such a letter without first consulting all the members. It was obvious to many that one person on the Standing Committee, who had left Christ Church and opposed the Scheme for demolition and re-building, had successfully persuaded the other members of the Committee to concur with his sentiments.

The debate lasted some twenty minutes and the outcome was quite satisfactory. The Synod voted on a resolution that the Rural

Dean should write a letter to the Bishop on behalf of the Synod, indicating that the majority of the members were in favour of the new Christ Church building.

Outside the church a number of members approached me. Some expressed incredulity that such a dastardly deed should be done behind the back of the members of the synod. If anything, I discovered far more support than had hitherto been the case, and so yet again, the devil had overplayed his hand!

Timothy Bigdon, the Financial Controller of the Diocese, had written to me on June 9th, in which he stated that the scheme in his professional judgement, was not viable! The two areas he was unhappy about were, the use of cheap labour from Kent Skills, and the reliance upon a Compulsory Purchase Order which, as yet, had not been brought to a satisfactory conclusion. We could put pressure on Robert Wickham to settle the CPO. However, this last alternative would not be easy, as it involved solicitors and the Land's Tribunal. Much more work needed to be done on our presentation to the Diocesan Board of Finance, but the sands of time were running out.

Chapter 13

Black Tuesday

The meeting of The Board of Finance was due to commence at 2:15 pm. Arriving early at Charing Cross, Dick and I headed towards the Houses of Parliament. We crossed the road under the lea of Westminster Abbey, turned a corner and arrived at Church House. We stood nervously on the pavement wondering how to spend the next half-an-hour, and decided to go to a small street restaurant, both to pray and to eat.

To me London always has a frantic atmosphere whether by day or night. Apart from Japanese visitors and French School parties, everyone walks quickly, cars drive faster and people eat as if there is no tomorrow; this little restaurant was no different. Even the food arrived before you had ordered it. As we sat down I observed some business men, official papers in one hand and eating a quick sandwich with the other. Dick and I were now part of this frenetic *milieu*.

I left Dick preparing our case and I went to the meeting. Church House is the centre of Church of England affairs, and once a year accommodates the churches parliament, the General Synod. The room in which we met was thirty feet long, with two polished tables extending almost the full length. The top table formed a U shape, while around the walls were paintings of important people who, at some stage, had led and coloured the Church of England's activity. I had always thought that Earl Grey was merely a posh name for a brand of tea until I saw this ermine-robbed figure gazing down on the assembled group of people. To be sure, Earl Grey had been a most distinguished gentleman.

At the invitation of the chairman, the Bishop opened the meeting in prayer before we began the business of the afternoon. A good deal of time was taken up with the budget. Glancing at my watch, I saw three-fifteen arrive, then four-fifteen. This meeting had become the longest in my four years of being a member. Not three hundred yards away, Big Ben struck four-thirty and two or three members got up to leave. I wondered about Dick sitting out in the corridor, and whether our item would ever be tabled. At precisely four-thirty-five the chairman introduced, 'Holy Trinity with Christ Church scheme.'

Prior to the meeting, the Diocesan Financial Controller, Mr. Timothy Bigden, had circulated members with his own assessment of the viability of the project, and it expressed his grave concerns. Dick was invited into the meeting, and at the invitation of the chairman, I stood up and gave a quick potted history, stating how much time and energy, plus expertise, had gone into ten years of preparing for this day. I expressed concern that we still needed some more time in order to make financial savings, but this was not possible due to the pressure to perform. I then handed over to Dick and he presented the financial case. I was confident that his presentation would influence the members. At Dick's conclusion a few more members got up to leave and Big Ben clanged five o'clock. It was decision time. Dick and I were asked to leave the room while the matter was debated. We walked towards the reception. The marble tiles of Church House in its 19th century regal splendour, old and distinguished, contrasted strongly with the tall lady in a turquoise mini-skirt at the reception. For a further twenty-five minutes we anxiously paced up and down, before being called back into the meeting.

As I sat down I glanced around the room, looking for some reaction. People were either looking at the ceiling, or nervously fumbling with papers — no one directly looked at me. This, was a bad sign. The Chairman spoke.

'John, thank you for your presentation, the committee have spent some time debating the issue and we have decided to send it back to the Pastoral Committee, and that's our decision.'

'Mr. Chairman, with all due respect, can I please ask the Bishop what are the implications of this decision?' I asked.

The Bishop replied, 'The new building scheme in Tunbridge

Wells has not received the approval of this committee and, as such, it is finished.'

I felt the blood drain from my face. I was both shocked, angry, and terribly hurt. My disappointment was overwhelming. The meeting closed with the Grace, and we all got up to leave. As I got to the door, a lady moved alongside me and gently gripped my hand.

'All is not lost,' she said.

Dick and I came out of Church House, walked across Parliament Square and waited to cross the road at the traffic signals. Norman Warren, the Archdeacon of Rochester came up along side.

'You must both be devastated,' he said. 'What magnificent church in England, including our cathedrals, had to have all the money up front before the work was commenced? On the strength of what happened today, St. Paul's Cathedral would never have been built!'

Norman disappeared into Westminster underground station and Dick and I walked along the Thames Embankment. It was now a bright day. We had started out with optimism when the day was overcast, and now we were leaving with disappointment while the weather was sunny. Was God trying to tell us something? Tourist buses were lined up, parked underneath the trees, and camera-clad people passed us by on their way to the most famous clock in the world. Still stunned into silence, we struggled for something useful to say, perhaps to salvage something from the meeting. We walked into Charing Cross Station concourse and I made my way to a telephone.

At the vicarage, a number of praying people had gathered and it was now time to inform them of the result.

'Christ Church Vicarage, can I help you?' Celia's bright and cheerful tone certainly contrasted with the emotions Dick and I were feeling.

'They have thrown it out, love. Lock, stock and barrel. Kaput, finish, finito.'

'Darling, you must feel devastated! How is Dick?'

'Punch drunk, like me. We are catching the five-forty-five, see you in an hour's time.'

I turned to Dick and said, 'All the congregation will know within the next quarter-of-an-hour.'

'If only we have been given more time John. Time to make more savings. Time to re-design the roof. Time to settle the Compulsory Purchase Order.'

On the train I sat next to the window. Within minutes a lady had sat opposite us. She turned out to be a Christian, and told us of her successful church in Hastings. The train pulled out of the station and rattled and squeaked its way to London Bridge. I cast my eyes to the skyline, and immediately noticed Canary Wharf on the new Docklands estate. Here was a multi-million pound building scheme.

'If the world can do it, so can God!' I thought. I felt sore with God, he had let us down. Eleven years of paperwork, hundreds of committees, thousands of miles travelling, an attic loaded with paperwork, and the services of the top experts in their field, but we had nothing to show for it.

After some twenty minutes the train pulled into Orpington Station. My thoughts wandered. It would be so easy to hand in my resignation and leave the Church of England. Celia and I could rent a little place in the country and get away from all the hurt. I didn't want to be a Christian any more. I didn't want to preach any more. I didn't want to talk about God any more. It was obvious prayer doesn't work.

The Vicarage was about seven minutes walk from Tunbridge Wells station. As we walked in Celia, Lesley and Jessie were seated around the kitchen table. We briefly gave a summary of the afternoon. Within an hour or so, a number of people rang the Vicarage to commiserate and the same question was repeated, 'Where do we go from here?

After tea Celia and I sat down and read Spurgeon's reading for June 15. 'Sarah said, God has brought me laughter, and everyone who hears about this [Isaac's birth] will laugh with me'. Spurgeon wrote the following: 'This day will I lift up psalms of triumph unto the Lord who has remembered my low estate, for my heart rejoiceth in the Lord; mine horn is exalted in the Lord; my mouth is enlarged over mine enemies, because I rejoice in thy salvation.'

In the light of what had happened there was little encouragement to laugh, yet clearly this was the will of the Lord for us, to laugh in the face of adversity, what a victorious note. The phone rang at 7.15 pm.

'Christ Church Vicarage.'

'John, bishop Michael here.'

'Good evening Bishop.'

'John, I just wanted to give you a call, knowing how disappointed you must be over the Board's decision this afternoon.'

I was immediately comforted by his concern, though the Lord knows I have always felt under pressure from the Bishop to perform.

'John, we all want to see a new church in Tunbridge Wells, so take the initiative and seek a new scheme, preferably with a different architect. Your present one will be tempted simply to look for savings and not look to a fresh start.'

'It's an enormous blow Michael. We have sacrificed hundreds of hours, mountains of paperwork and worked our way through so many meetings with all the bureaucracy, not to mention the expenditure of £350,000.'

'The further delay in building the new church will adversely affect the present church membership and begin to tell on your health,' said Michael. 'If you go back to the drawing board now, you could have a new set of plans before the Diocesan Pastoral Committee within a year.'

The Bishop was right, we would painfully go back to the drawing board.

'Alright, we will go for it, but I don't mind telling you there is little enthusiasm at the present time.'

That evening Celia and I, in need of comfort and encouragement, went to see Norman and Yvonne Warren at the Archdeacon's house in Rochester. The Archdeaconry is within the cathedral and Kings School complex of buildings. It is an enormous house with truly a regal entrance and wide imposing hall. Norman was a gifted songwriter and Yvonne a valuable resource in marriage counselling. These people exuded love and concern and a great deal of compassion. Throughout our short stay, they both assured us that this was of the Lord and therefore would succeed despite the enormous opposition to it.

'You can build a magnificent church with a million pounds,' said Norman with a high degree of excitement.

'Then we must go for it' I replied. 'After all, God has already built the congregation and that was the most important part of the whole building procedure.'

Celia nodded at my remark. After a prayer time together we left the Archdeaconry. The cool evening air somehow seemed charged with positive particles. I knew we both felt content and shared our feelings journeying back to Royal Tunbridge Wells. Celia and I retired late. We lay in the darkness for some twenty minutes. I could hold my disappointment no longer. As I lay on the pillow the tears started to run down my face. I tried to sob without letting on, but the shaking of my shoulders told Celia I was in the depth of disappointment. She inched towards me and putting her hands upon my shoulders said, 'Darling, I feel for you. Please don't cry.'

But right now, that was the one thing I wanted to do. I blurted out, 'God doesn't love us any more! We've got it all wrong! We have expended three hundred and fifty thousand pounds and haven't moved a solitary brick!'

We both lay quietly for a bit, and eventually I drifted off to sleep.

Thankfully June 19 was a hot, clear-skyed sunny day and as a belated birthday present Lesley had bought me a ticket for the Biggin Hill Air Show. Biggin Hill airfield has an almost legendary story, it being one of the many war time stations. But now the RAF had left. A Russian mature student had come to stay with us for six months to learn our language, and as a committed Christian he would learn more theology if he mastered English. He and I set off for the airshow. From the time of leaving the vicarage, to arriving at the airfield, Alex showed all the signs of an excited five year old going to his first party!

Before I had a chance to lock the car, Alex was striding off. We promised to meet at the Commentary Box around 1 pm for lunch. One memorable picture I have was seeing Alex standing on the edge of the crowd watching two crack Russian pilots during a great aerobatic display. Soon after they landed they were driven in an open topped vehicle down the full length of the crowd . Alex was close to jumping up and down, and shouted something in Russian as they passed by. I was thrilled for him, because this was one occasion when our pattern of life and affluence, which had so over-awed him, was in a sense equalled by this magnificent display. This outing with Alex was, for me, a welcome respite in an altogether gloomy scenario.

One thing I was not looking forward to was announcing to the congregation the following Sunday the decision of the Diocesan Board of Finance, a day which in my mind, would become known as 'Black Tuesday'. In my prayers, before the morning service, I turned to my Bible and, in quite a determined mood, opened at the book of Habakkuk 2:1-3.

> *'I will stand at my watch and station myself on the ramparts; I will look to see what he will say to me, and what answer I am to give to this complaint. Then the Lord replied, 'Write down the revelation and make it plain on tablets so that a herald may run with it. For the revelation awaits an appointed time; it speaks of the end and will not prove false. Though it linger, wait for it; it will certainly come and will not delay.'*

I had no time to think through the context of these verses, all I knew was that they spoke to me and that I would need to pass this on to the congregation. Members of the Church Council had already shared the news of this enormous set back with friends and congregational members, and even before the morning service commenced many people expressed how devastated they were at this enormous disappointed. I saw faces show incredulity. The atmosphere was filled with sadness, heartache and many tears as hope and expectations were crushed again. This made my job of leading worship and singing praises to the Lord much more difficult. My only consolation was this word from Habakkuk. I would have to proclaim it as a distinct prophetic insight that the Lord was having his way with us, and building his church in a way we did not understand but later would fully appreciate.

On top of all this the doctors still had not sorted Pym out. She was still in a critical condition and her new heart pacemaker was causing problems, and so I was without her in the church office.

Almost two weeks later the PCC and I met Peter Law, the Diocesan Secretary, and Archdeacon Richard Mason in the Parish Hall. Doom and gloom pervaded the group of people that met before the two officials. After I prayed, the Archdeacon assessed the present situation. He made mention of the fact that plans for a new church to replace Holy Trinity and Christ Church in the heart of the town centre in Tunbridge Wells had been going on for some twenty odd years. He expressed the anxiety that the recent decision of the Diocesan Board of Finance had made upon both the incumbent and the congregation in general. Notwithstanding the set-back, it was still feasible that the building scheme should go ahead on a less grandiose scale. 'After all,' he reminded us, 'You can do an awful lot with one million pounds, and as God gave the vision, then he will see it through.'

Peter Law followed the Archdeacon in making mention of the fact that the recession that the country was now going through did not help our cause. The forward funding for the shopping precinct, expected to be £1.3 million, was now no longer available. He did insist, however, that such a new scheme should be within the cash limits available, and that it was the wish of the Bishop that a new architect be appointed as soon as was reasonable.

'I do not think we should attempt to do anything for the next three to four months. I believe that we need time to pray, to reflect, and to understand the way in which God is dealing with us,' I said.

Richard Aydon, a member of the PCC, concurred with me, and was anxious that we should not enter into any negotiations for some considerable time. The meeting concluded with the two officials leaving and the PCC were left to cogitate.

The air of gloom was only punctuated by the thought of starting the process of building a new church from scratch. An air of resignation permeated every brain, and the overall consensus of opinion was to move away from the whole issue and rest awhile. Our hurts could only be dealt with by the passage of time. Life would go on, and we covenanted to pray that God would continue to guide us.

The following day I rang Brenda Davison, our Architect, to inform her that the DBF had thrown out the scheme in its entirety and I was now under orders to appoint a new architect as she would be tempted to reduce the scheme, and what was needed was a whole new fresh mind. Brenda, as Graham, was totally devastated and it was with great reluctance that I confirmed this the following day in a letter to them.

Within three days Celia and I found ourselves journeying to

Bournemouth to attend Stephen's graduation ceremony. We reflected, going down the M3, that it must be one of the hottest days of the year. Our thoughts were with Miles at Bethany School, who would not have any family supporters at his Speech Day, though he did not seem too disturbed by the fact that, on this occasion, it was more important to be with Stephen at Moorlands Bible College. It was a proud Mum and Dad that saw Stephen get his graduation certificate. After tea, and congratulations all round, we headed back to Tunbridge Wells, collecting Miles *en route*.

The following day another happy event was the celebration of Russell's 21st birthday. Quite a number of his college friends came to the Vicarage and Lesley Still baked a special cake. By this time the following year he would, hopefully, have his degree in geography from Hull University. 'What of his future?' I wondered. He could be the one son who could follow in his father's footsteps as a Church of England minister. There is no question in my mind that without a clear and definite calling by God, there is no way he would survive such a vocation. One may be one's own boss in parochial terms, and therefore there is a degree of freedom, yet the Christian conscience can be a terrible task master. And woe betide if he chooses to marry, and ends up marrying the wrong girl! His wife too must be called to ministry.

'Orangeman's Day', July 12th, was the day chosen to see two churches in our diocese that the Bishop and Archdeacon had recommended as those buildings roughly in the similar cost bracket comparable to the money we possessed, ie, £750,000 to £800,000. At ten o'clock in the morning John Kain, Dick Warren and I met Bob Groves, Vicar of Anerley, and with some pride, he showed us around the building. For me the building was unduly complicated with lots of walls, and what appeared to be an unusual design around a central worship area. We were soon on the road again, now making for the church of St. Justus, Rochester, where John Lawrence was the vicar. We were met and conducted around the church by the administrator. The building was a bright, open design with lots of windows letting through a good deal of natural light.

Journeying back we reflected upon our visit to the two churches. The quality of the brickwork at Anerley was far superior to that of St. Justus, and this was something that was quite obviously important, particularly for Royal Tunbridge Wells and the High Street location. We needed a quality building.

My next day off was grey and overcast. Celia and I thought it a good idea to spend the time at home. I bought a book of graph paper, and in the afternoon I spent time drawing the church plan to scale, and had a rough idea of how the finished scheme should look. At the main front of the building there should be two shops at the ground floor, with a generous double glass door opening. This would lead into a narthex, (the foyer of a church) off to the left and to the right there would be the church office, committee room, toilet facilities, and a small chapel. A further set of doors would lead into the worship area, with a generous auditorium seating three hundred people. I saw a high dias, some twenty-four inches above the floor level. Upstairs there would be Sunday School classrooms clustered around a parish hall. The car park to the church would surround the building on two sides. Celia and I spent the early part of the evening revising things, particularly the kitchen, and making sure that there were adequate facilities for the disabled, which would include a lift to the upper floor.

Within the days that followed, I shared the drawings with a number of people, and they all added their little bit of alteration. But the basic design, all agreed, was simple and uncomplicated.

John Kain had suggested that we draw up the names of three architectural practices. The three architects were, David Grayston, Fred Briars and Ray Woodward. On July 19th we met each in turn. We made available the model of the previous design, and I produced my sketch drawings as to how I saw the building. At the end of the day, we agreed to meet again in early November, the summer would give time for each architect to interpret the vision. My holidays would include RAF Coltishall with the Air Cadets, followed by a two week holiday in Minorca.

My four days at RAF Coltishall proved to be a time of great relaxation. The high point was a flight in a chipmunk, a single-engine aircraft with two seats fore and aft, with dual controls. Having got myself trussed-up with all the usual gear, plus helmet, headphones and parachute, I went out to the aircraft. The pilot was a highly trained ex-senior officer, now semi-retired. Nearly all of these pilots would have flown some very sophisticated aircraft in their day. I walked out to the plane and climbed aboard. After a quick 'Good afternoon' to the 'driver', we sped down the runway, and took off over the countryside.

The now familiar conversation took place. Name...? Where do you live...? Have you flown before...? etc, etc.

'What would you like us to do?' he asked.

My reply was swift and had been regularly rehearsed: 'Can we loop the loop?'

'Yes, of course,' came the reply, 'But we'll need to get to at least four thousand feet!'

I watched as the joystick was pulled back, and kept an eye on the altimeter. We were now climbing steadily. At four thousand feet the aircraft levelled out.

'Are you okay?' asked the pilot.

'Yes I'm okay,' I replied.

Ray gave the run through on what would happen. 'I shall push the stick well forward, putting the aircraft in a dive. I shall then pull the stick right back and we shall climb and do a complete somersault. Is that clear?'

'Yes, I'm looking forward to this!' I replied.

'Will you check with me that the horizon is completely clear of aircraft — remember that there are four others up at the same time!'

We both glanced around the aircraft.

'All clear?' he asked. I switched on the intercom near my nose.

'Yes all clear,' I said.

He shouted, 'Tally-ho!'

The stick went forward, the revs lifted, and we were heading to the ground at a forty-five degree angle. Within less than a minute the stick came back fully and the plane rose into a massive arc. I felt the G-force pushing me right back into my seat. Then the sky became the land, and the land became the sky! We reached the top of the circle and shot round again. It was confusing and somewhat disorienting, but most exhilarating. We levelled off at some two-and-a-half thousand feet.

'Are you okay?' asked Ray.

I switched on my intercom, 'Yes I'm fine. That was absolutely fantastic!'

Back came an immediate reply. 'Now it's your turn! Watch your altimeter and climb to four thousand feet. You take control,' he said. I replied with the regulation, 'I have control!'

For the first time I find myself in charge of an aeroplane, and apart from the rudder bar, I controlled the aircraft from the lever in front of me. I pulled the stick back, climbed to four thousand feet and levelled off.

'Now remember what to do — Stick full forward, and when I shout "back" pull the stick as far back as you can and, with a bit of luck, we shall loop the loop again!'

I repeated the whole exercise. On completion he said, 'We pulled four 'G' that time... That was a tight circle!'

We headed back to the airfield. Another of my little dreams had come true. This was a far cry from all the anxiety over buildings.

November arrived, and in the first week we met the three architects. All submitted good overall schemes for the new church and church hall. However, David Grayston's drawing appeared to be the nearest to that which we had sketched earlier, so he was given the appointment. The following morning I woke about 8:30 am and put on the television by my bedside for a time check. There was a programme featuring the work of the well known Scandinavian architect Hennig Larsen. Much of his work is in the middle-east, and the film showed examples of his use of natural sunlight and strategic use of internal water fountains. Within the hour I had rung John Kain and he had informed me that a colleague had a video of Hennig Larsen's work. Within a matter of days a number of us watched this video. Here were features that could very well be expressed in our new building. I rang David Grayston and we talked at length about Larsen's work and he promised that he would incorporate such features in his design. By early December we had met the new design team. We all lived within a radius of fifteen miles, which would make life easier for regular meetings. December 17th saw us meeting at the architect's practice for Christmas cocktails, and it was quite clear that we were all going to get on exceptionally well with each other.

As a congregation we were now heading into our eleventh year and, so far, not a brick removed or laid in the High Street. The money we had lost was substantial, and I mused whether God counted that as important. Should I have resigned at the failure of the earlier scheme? Somehow, the vision given to me way back in Liverpool would not allow me to pack-up now. God had built his church — the people — and now we needed to be housed, but how long was this going to take? If the enthusiasm of the new team was of any significance, the present plans would succeed, and hopefully by 1995 we would be well under way in building the new church.

I asked God, 'Why was it taking so long — Where does my stamina come from? Who gave me the "stickability" to stay the course? Could I continue to carry others with me?'

I reflected upon a sermon back in August, preached by the Right Rev. Ivan Neill, Provost of Sheffield and former Chaplain-General to the army. He was preaching at All Saints, Crowborough, East Sussex, on the evening of August 8th, and while I could not remember much of what he said, a phrase kept repeating itself as he addressed the congregation: 'Stay with it... Endure... Be consistent... Stay the course.'

This sounded like an echo of Martin Luther: 'Behold, here I stand, I can do no other'.

Chapter 14

Cooden reflections

It was precisely ten past seven when I left the vicarage. I stopped at the entrance of the drive to check my gear: good walking boots, special hiking socks, and a dark green showerproof jacket. Armed with my shooting stick, I set off down Farmcombe Road on my sponsored walk.

The sky was overcast for May although the sun could be seen as an orange haze towards the east. I shared some thoughts with the Lord, asking for fair weather, the strength to do the trip and safety while walking along narrow country lanes. I was certain the sponsorship would raise more than twelve hundred pounds. I walked with a confident swagger, sliding my shooting stick through my fingers, and wondering if around the next bend a congregational member or two might surprise me, having volunteered to join me on this thirty-mile hike to the south coast.

Leaving Forest Road and heading out towards Wadhurst, some seven miles away, at last I was on my own, civilisation behind me. Now I had time to think and reflect concerning events earlier in the year. The ordination of women had upset about a third of the Church of England's clergy, and a number of my colleagues had left the ministry. Added to this, there was an increasing debate about the acceptability of priests who were practising homosexuals.

On the local scene, the new Calvary Free Church had been opened by Michael Turnbull, which I had attended with Robert Wickham. We both congratulated the pastor and his people at the reception time. In seeking compensation for the compulsory purchase order of Crabb Hall, we had both fought long and hard alongside

Derek Martin, Senior Elder of Calvary Free, for adequate compensation for our tenants, and a proper financial arrangement for our loss of the building, in favour of the Royal Victoria Shopping Mall.

The day prior to the CPO enforcement Robert paid a visit to the vicarage, and we both told our stories of how we had attempted to get keys to Crabb Hall.

'I am concerned John, that we do not have all the dimensions of the building, both internally and externally. I have brought a measure and pad complete with basic drawing, do you think we could break into the building?'

'Yes I think we could' I responded, and with that I went down to the garage. We both set off for Crabb Hall with various tools, including a pickaxe. It was a late sunny morning and we parked the car outside the building. I took out the pickaxe and we examined the door of the hall, which was firmly locked.

'There is nothing for it Robert, we have to break the door down!'

Robert nervously looked around to see if the coast was clear.

'Go ahead then.'

I pulled back the pickaxe, but then spotted a police car coming up the road. I threw the axe under the car, turned round, and tried to look like a quantity surveyor eyeing up the building. Robert spent the moments peering at an empty page in his pad. With the police car gone, and two swipes with the pickaxe, the doors flung open and we were in. With some haste Robert and I started to measure the rooms one by one. Some of the upstairs rooms were small and musty. There was a youth hall with straight walls and no windows. Looking at a forlorn hymn-book lying on the floor, I heard a voice somewhere in the bowels of the building. I noticed that Robert was missing. Following the sound of his voice, I found him at the foot of the stairs. By the light of a small torch he was taking off his shoes and socks.

'Robert, is that really necessary? The building is not that holy!' I said with some mirth in my voice.

'Yes' he replied, 'We must get all the dimensions for valuation purposes.'

Robert disappeared into the gloom, paddling in ten inches of water. I made stepping stones with some bricks I found in a corner. Fifteen minutes later we returned upstairs, and left for the vicarage. After coffee Robert got in his car, saying, 'This is all the evidence we require.'

The Diocesan Advisory Committee had temporarily set our scheme back, but in the words of the chairman, Rev. Michael Hodge, this was merely a hiccup, and minor problems would soon be overcome. Robert Wickham had continued to lobby the District Valuation officer in Tunbridge Wells to seek fair compensation for the loss of Crabb Hall. This whole matter seemed to be dragging on interminably. The original arrangement was, that as part of the compensation package, Calvary Church would be given a shell of a building which they would have to fit out. However, the new pastor, David Adkins, had challenged the Borough Council that the church did not have enough money to equip the building, and so were further compensated to the tune of £300,000. The church held a ninety-nine year lease, and the Borough Council held the freehold. But what monies had been given to them, it would appear, were at the expense of us getting proper compensation at Christ Church. Going to the Lands Tribunal would concentrate the minds of the DVO and Borough Council, and hopefully rule in favour of proper compensation.

One man who had been able to throw a good deal of light on the subject was Bill Rees, a member of the well known Rees family (Tom and Dick Rees had been evangelists, Michael Rees was General of the Church Army and Jennifer Rees-Larcombe had written books on healing, and been miraculously healed in 1993). Bill, in the mind of Robert Wickham, was a foremost authority on Lands Tribunal matters. Indeed, at one stage Robert stated that he had written the 'bible' of the Lands Tribunal. And so the three of us had met in late March, in the Sevenoaks office of Ibbett Moseley. At one point I asked Bill outright what our chances were of succeeding in getting a good settlement through challenging Tunbridge Wells Borough Council in the Lands Tribunal. Bill had quoted two other cases in the south-east involving compensation to churches where the settlement had been generous.

'Your case in the heart of Tunbridge Wells stands a good chance of succeeding and I will encourage Robert to pursue the matter right up to the court.'

Continuing my walk and after a brief stop in Wadhurst, Jessie providing coffee and Veronica massaging my feet, I duly set off again.

'Next stop, Stonegate, and then Burwash,' I said with some triumph in my voice.

I waved them goodbye, and set off towards Ticehurst. I found this stretch to be a little dangerous, for after the last house in Wadhurst the pavements disappeared and I was constantly having to leave the road for the grass verge.

'Beep, beep!' The ladies passed by. After Stonegate it was open country. This proved to be a very wet walk indeed. We had had a lot of rain. Small streams had flooded and the land was saturated. At one point the cows had created nothing short of a mire. Before entering the woods, I took off my green jacket and wrapped it around my waist. A gentleman was coming from the opposite direction with two dogs. I casually remarked on the wet conditions, and he replied, 'It's a darn sight wetter further down!'

I began to whistle a series of Sousa marches, which encouraged my step considerably. I then began to sing my own Benedicite: 'Oh! all ye works of the Lord, bless ye the Lord.'

Then, looking round, I continued: 'Oh! all ye bluebells, bless ye the Lord... Oh! all ye cows, bless ye the Lord... Praise him and magnify him forever. Oh! all ye trees, bless ye the Lord... Oh! all ye birds, bless ye the Lord... Oh! all ye rabbits, bless ye the Lord... Praise him and magnify him forever.'

In the valley before Burwash I met a middle-aged couple from London, who accompanied me across the river valley and up through the woods to the village of Burwash. On leaving the woods I displayed my horticultural ignorance, by remarking on the presence of a lovely bluebell, to which the lady replied, 'That, my dear, is an orchid!'

I blushed and made some feeble excuse. We arrived at the village, a delightful place, set on a hill in the county of East Sussex. It sits on a ridge and properties either side of the main road face an extensive dip into the adjacent countryside. Two churches, a couple of pubs, a garage or two and some period buildings, made up this delightful village. I said goodbye to my friends and left the village heading south. The early morning haze lifted and the sun warmed my path for the next ten miles.

At one point on the road, I heard a distinct rat-tat-tat in a tree some one hundred and fifty yards ahead: a woodpecker. I had seen many pictures but never a live one. I crept quietly and gingerly until I was within seven yards of the tree. The drilling stopped. I froze, and for a long minute total silence. To my dismay the woodpecker had flown.

Perhaps, due to the silence, a baby rabbit appeared from the hedgerow. Our eyes met as if in greeting, then it shot away into a burrow.

Some two miles further on I encountered a field of frisky bullocks; all were anxious to greet me. Within minutes, these were joined by a whole herd, who positively galloped across the field to see what all the fuss was about. A long climb up towards the British Gypsum Works found me casting off my top jacket and light pullover. I reckoned that by now I had walked thirteen miles. My lower back was now beginning to burn with pain. Could I carry on much longer? At the half way point, I turned a right hand bend in the road, and spotted a familiar car parked in a lay-by. Jessie had already set out the lunch plates, and provided cold chicken legs with salad and some sliced ham.

'Before you think about lunch John,' Veronica started, 'I suggest we give you a good oiling and greasing!'

I replied, 'What a good idea... my lower back is in a lot of pain.'

'Strip off to the waist,' she dictated.

'What on earth are you going to do?' I asked with some surprise.

'I'm going to massage your back into shape,' she said.

From the back of the car she took out a thick blanket and laid it on the road. At least I'm not going to get run over, I thought.

After the massage and with lunch over, I was back on the road. Within half-an-hour I had reached an observatory, and from here on it was all downhill to the coast. Thanks to Veronica, and the Lord above, I was in no discomfort. On an easy stretch of straight flat road, I heard the Beep! Beep! of my own car. Celia was at the wheel, accompanied by Leslie, Sally and Audrey Danby. She stopped the car some half a mile ahead, and walked back towards me. She greeted me with a hug.

'Darling, what a long way you've walked. How do you feel?' she asked.

'Fit as a fiddle,' I said. 'South Coast here I come!'

We walked along hand in hand for a while, then she returned to the car and the lane became quiet again.

I was determined that ten percent of the money raised would go to the Gahini hospital building project. From the earliest days of raising money for the new church I had advocated giving ten percent of the money raised to overseas missions. So far we had given £28,000 towards the rebuilding and reordering of the hospital in Rwanda. During this time we had met and loved Rob and Tricia Wilson, the doctor and his wife who had spent a number of years at the hospital. In recent days it had been a great joy to our congregation to receive the first pictures of the new building work, and for us all there was a deep satisfaction.

By three o'clock in the afternoon, I estimated the total distance was about thirty miles. After a further drink of glucose and a chocolate biscuit, I pushed on to the coast. By five o'clock I was half a mile short of Cooden. Celia had parked the car at the home of Dr Sheena Ashby and walked back towards me.

'Darling, we are all so proud of you! You have done extremely well... And all this in aid of the new church fund!'

By now I was aching all over, yet also quite stimulated. I had a real sense of achievement. Within ten minutes we were sitting in Sheena's little cottage, enjoying tea and cakes.

'Sheena,' I asked, 'How far is it to the coast from here?'

'Exactly one mile,' she returned.

'Then I could have done the thirty miles after all!'

Celia interjected, 'You've done enough for one day!'

Back home, on Monday morning I felt well enough to respond to Celia's suggestion that I mow the lawn. It so happens that we have not one lawn mower, but two. The latter machine was a very old Atco, given to us by our friend Jessie. It sat upright, was cranked by a handle, and by closing 'this' and opening 'the other', one could get it to work perfectly well. It also possessed a dangerous looking fly-wheel with an antique clutch arrangement.

For the first two cuts, I used our Mountfield lawnmower, a rotary blade which proved very successful. Having put this lawn-mower to one side, I then proceeded to get Jessie's Atco out of the shed. On top of the machine there was a small plastic bag, within which I discovered the instruction booklet, a spare plug, and a spanner. I quickly read the instructions, put them back in the plastic bag and placed them on a shelf in the shed.

'Now my old beauty — let's see what you're made of!'

I opened the petrol cap, threw a knob to one side, and took the crank handle, placed it in the side of the machine and, swung it round. The machine replied, 'Putt, putt, putt, putt...' and then it gave a gasp. I adjusted a lever and swung it a second time. This time it fired and, with blue smoke blowing, I had the engine ticking over smoothly. Unaware of the idiosyncrasies of the machine, I pointed it in the most appropriate direction and threw the clutch arrangement onto the fly-wheel. The machine immediately lurched forward, with me following a close second. We were both heading across the lawn at breakneck speed and with no way to avoid a rapidly approaching wall. With a swift swing of my arm, I did a 180 degree turn, and at a ferocious pace headed back towards the garden shed. Panicking, I pulled the lever. Instead of the motor stopping, it increased the power! I was now at a running pace.

'Tally-ho, the machine doesn't need me!' I thought.

A quick flick of the wrist, and I swung the machine back the way we had come. By now I was running alongside the machine, having let go of the handle, and cut off the petrol supply at the appropriate tap. The machine carried on for a few more yards and then, thankfully, stopped. I glared at it with a mixture of fear and unbelief.

I sat down on the grass and as I did so I heard a peel of laughter from the direction of the house. Celia, with tears running down her face, was completely beside herself. She could not bring herself to speak. The laughing took over. She walked down the garden and with both arms around my neck she whispered, 'Love you!'

As I placed this beast back in the shed I reflected, 'I'd prefer a twenty-nine mile walk any day than being taken on a race with an errant lawn-mower.'

That evening I read *Daily Light*, and believed again in the humour of God. It read: 'Let us lay aside every weight, and the sin which so easily besets us, and let us run with patience the race that is set before us, looking unto Jesus the author and finisher of our faith.'

July 6th was a hot, sunny morning. Celia and I had planned a trip to Hull University for Russell's graduation. A day earlier he had turned twenty-two years of age and had completed his degree in Geography.

Speeding north, we reflected on a further frustration to the new building scheme. The Diocesan Advisory Committee, a committee of specialists predominantly covering historical aspects of church buildings, needed to be convinced that the old building was now beyond repair. Consequently, I went to see the secretary at Church House. She convinced me that objections could be met with a little co-operation, patience and mutual agreement. Nevertheless, it was another hiccup we could do without!

We arrived at Russell's hall of residence, and after settling in we walked the campus. The following day, at Hull city civic centr,e Russell received his degree. Celia and I were both very proud parents, witnessing something very special. With cocktails in the afternoon, and a dinner in the evening, the two day event finished with Celia and I helping to clear out the home Russell had been renting in his last year.

Nicola's graduation was a less regal affair and held an atmosphere of informality. The venue for her award was in a large marquee in the grounds of Hadlow College of Agriculture and Horticulture. The temperature was in the nineties, and not a few collars were undone and ties discarded. The ladies however, relished the idea of enjoying their summer dresses, and filled the occasion with colour, matched appropriately by bouquets of flowers, arranged by the 'Hortics.'

Nicola was all aglow and duly queued up to receive her certificate. As she made to the stage, a small cheer rang out, and with a beaming smile she received her award. With a few tears of goodbye, she left her colleagues and returned home with us. With the exception of Christopher, we were now a complete family again. Within a further two weeks we flew out to the island of Minorca, taking Miles and Kerry with us.

The sunny summer continued into the first weeks of September. During this period I received a letter from the diocese asking for information regarding the old Christ Church. Amused by this latest enquiry, and wondering who required the information for whom, I rang the assistant secretary David Gater.

'John, it would appear that someone has threatened to take the Archdeacon to court over the demolition of the present Christ Church building, and therefore it would be useful to have as much information as possible.'

'I can share with you David,' I began, 'that Christ Church was never built as an ecclesiastical structure. The original plan was to build a Victorian style music hall.'

'Oh! Now that's very interesting,' he interjected.

I continued, 'It would appear that the builder was sent to

Tasmania by the English courts for breaking various building regulations as existed at that time, and there were, in the building, many structural defects which concerned the Parochial Church Council so much so that they wished to demolish the building fourteen years after it was finished by a local vicar. The first incumbent, William Franklin, spent some three-thousand pounds; and thereby completed the building as a church, hence the fact that there is no foundation stone. There is, however, in the foundations of the present building a time capsule possessing certain documents and coins of the realm, dated 1835.'

'John I will pass the information on to the Archdeacon, and no doubt we can correspond further on this matter over the next couple of weeks,' he replied.

I replaced the phone, and said aloud to myself, 'The devil is still opposing this scheme.'

It had been announced in the press that with the retirement of David Jenkins, a very liberal and radical Bishop of Durham, his position would be taken by the Bishop of Rochester, Rt. Reverend Michael Turnbull. This would be a step up for Michael, for Durham held a very senior position in the hierarchy of Bishops. He accepted the appointment and my last glimpse of the Bishop and his wife Brenda was to see them both standing at the main door of the cathedral. Dressed in his robes together with his mitre, he looked all of seven foot tall as Brenda stood by his side holding his hand.

Despite the fact that Michael had upset me a few times, nevertheless these moments were outweighed by the love and the firmness of a man in high office who took his pastorship of the diocese seriously. The burning question now on the minds of many was, 'Who will take his place, and of what calibre will that man be?'

By the end of September, the Pastoral Committee of the diocese had met and discussed the scheme yet again. It was approved by the committee, subject to representations being made by various parties. Four members of the committee were to examine these recommendations and report their findings to the next meeting in February. This, I thought, would be a mere formality!

Chapter 15

We cried in the cathedral

It was 8:50 am on the morning of February 16th, 1995. I was quietly sitting at the breakfast table and was occupied with the morning's mail. I went into the study to collect my papers, and once everything was in my briefcase, I kissed Celia goodbye, and made off for Rochester and the Pastoral Committee Meeting. As I drove along, I was quite confident that the item on the agenda for our new church was a simple confirmation of the decision made last September, and now with a positive decision, the end was in sight.

At the meeting Michael Hodge, the Rector of Bidborough, sat on my left, and a chap I didn't know sat to my right. I was disappointed that my Archdeacon, Richard Mason, was not present. I was a good deal more comforted when Norman Warren, the Archdeacon of Rochester, came in. Our new Bishop, Michael Nazir-Ali began the meeting with prayer. At 11:20 am, the Bishop introduced the Christ Church item. Peter Law, the Diocesan Secretary, brought us up to date. He reminded us that the Committee had approved the scheme, subject to representations being made to all interested parties. Those to be consulted would include Archdeacon Mason, the Lay Chairman of the Deanery Synod (David Webster), the Rural Dean, (the Reverend Bob Whyte), the Church Pastoral Aid Society Patronage Board, the PCC of Christ Church, and myself. Four members of the committee were chosen to examine these representations and report to the committee. This they had done, reporting back in the affirmative, and now the matter should go before the Diocesan Board of Finance to clarify the costing of the scheme and give approval.

However, the Bishop chose to examine the two lengthy letters opposing the scheme. It was quite obvious to me, and to the others present, that coming from the same church, and historically opposing the scheme over many years, that there had been a concerted action to frustrate the re-building of Christ Church by the writers of these two letters.

The time dragged by and the meeting began to get silly as some of the basics that we had dealt with earlier were now coming back to a revised membership. We were covering old ground yet again. I could not believe my ears. The whole matter of the churches in Tunbridge Wells town centre was still in the melting pot after some twenty-seven years, and it appeared that the Church of England was incapable of making a binding decision, here was a clear example of a circum-bureacratic process. To my dismay, my best ally of the scheme, Norman Warren, got up to leave to attend his son's graduation.

'I'll get killed if I don't attend this one!' he commented as he got up to leave.

Chris Collins spoke out of sheer frustration having followed the progress of the scheme since 1983.

'Bishop,' he began, 'With all due respect to you, and to the new members of this committee, we are going over old ground yet again. We are spending far too many hours discussing the building when we should be listening to what the Holy Spirit of God is saying to us regarding this very active and vibrant congregation.'

The Suffragan Bishop, Brian Smith spoke out. 'If we don't proceed, then we have to meet the cost of the demolition of this building, and I'm concerned whether there is enough money to proceed with a new building.'

'That,' I replied, 'Is a matter for the Diocesan Board of Finance, and all the necessary figures will be demonstrated on that occasion…'

'…With supporting documentation,' the Bishop interjected.

I thought, 'Does this man not trust us?'

The third degree interrogation continued. We had now been talking for some thirty-five minutes. I whispered to Michael Hodge, 'We're going to be here until two o'clock this afternoon!'

The Bishop now desired to place a resolution to the committee.

A quick glance around the room revealed very few allies that I could rely upon. Many members were new and were unfamiliar with the long process we had been through to get this far. The resolution read: 'That this committee approves of the scheme, subject to the Diocesan Board of Finance being satisfied that the new building is financially viable, after which the Bishop will send the scheme to the Church Commissioners.'

'All those in favour,' directed the Bishop.

Eight hands went up. We were seventeen voting members. This could only mean there would be nine against. My heart sank. I whispered under my breath, 'Over to you God.'

'And those against?'

Seven.

'Abstentions?'

Two.

I breathed a huge sigh of relief and whispered to myself. 'Please Lord, don't do that again to me. That was too close for comfort!'

I glanced at my watch. The time was 11:50 am. The voting complete, the Bishop sat silently in his chair, but then made a startling comment.

'This vote is not sufficiently conclusive. I would like a straw vote.'

Michael Hodge then challenged the Bishop: 'On what resolution would we take a straw vote?'

I interrupted, 'If all members were present Bishop, including my own Archdeacon and the Archdeacon which has just left the meeting, then the voting would be much more persuasive.'

'But they are not present in the meeting,' the Bishop responded, 'Even though they may be in favour of the scheme.'

'Bishop we have taken a vote. It is in favour of the scheme. It is a majority decision, and it must now go before the Diocesan Board of Finance,' Michael Hodge added decisively.

The Bishop concurred and moved on to the next item on the agenda.

The meeting ended at 1:47 pm. Chris Collins made a comment that the process was like having a needle stuck on a gramophone.

'We are now on to our third Bishop,' he said. We left Church House and stood outside in the bright afternoon sunshine. I had never seen a February like this. Temperatures in the mid-fifties Fahrenheit and daffodils breaking out everywhere. I took a very deep breath and sighed, and walked back to the car. With no little delight, we may have won the day, but it was quite clear to me that the opposition would continue right up to the Privy Council, and we were still in for a long, hard fight.

I drove away from the cathedral precinct for a couple of miles and stopped at a garage. I picked up some petrol and a sandwich, then spotted a pay-phone. I rang Celia.

'Darling where are you?' she asked.

'The meeting has just concluded. I'm at a garage.'

'How did it go?' she enquired.

I quickly related the happenings of the morning, and then found my voice breaking up. I couldn't speak any more. Tears were welling up... Celia whispered down the phone, 'Come home darling, come home...'

After reporting the days events to the Prayer Group, we had our evening meal and, being my day off, we thought we might go out for a walk. The weather was atrocious, and walking was just not a possibility. At eight o'clock the phone rang.

'Dad, Chris here... Well, I've done it!'

'You've popped the question then?'

'Yes,' he replied, 'Claire and I are announcing our engagement!'

My thoughts shot back to two weeks earlier when we had discussed their future together, and having allayed something of his fears, he was more reassured that the Christian parameters that governed his parents successful marriage could, and should, be his and Claire's as well. I was confident that he would do the right thing. This was a bright and satisfying moment. I shouted to Celia, and she spoke to Claire and congratulated them personally.

Within days I had spoken to my Archdeacon Richard Mason and, quite clearly upset concerning the way the meeting had gone, he said he would raise the matter with the Bishop at their next meeting. Despite worries regarding the machinations of the established church, we were nevertheless continuing to discuss the new design with the architect, and had now appointed Gleeds, who had offices in

Tunbridge Wells, as our new Quantity Surveyors. On the latter's advice we had gone out to tender to six contractors, and on March 10th we met to open the contract prices. The lowest price came from BMP with the easily memorable price of £1,234,567.89.

Throughout the following week people kept enquiring as to how the meeting had progressed. I tried to keep a bright countenance about it all, but with all this bureaucratic bungling I was beginning to lose faith in the church I was brought up in, and basically loved.

One aspect of this whole saga troubled me. In previous days I had been reassured that there is a biblical precedence for praying against one's enemies. The enemies of our scheme were very verbal and active. The great puzzle of all was that so-called Christians were actually opposed to the progress, and indeed existence, of the congregation that had been so faithful. Could I bring myself to pray effectively against the enemy? I was fully aware that we wrestle not against flesh and blood. I had never been offended by a thumb, a toe-nail, an eye ball or a spleen, but I was aware that Satan can manipulate people against the will of God.

'Lord what do I pray… How do I pray concerning this matter?'

I was lead to open my Bible at Psalm 109. As I read this psalm, I began to feel that David, being pursued by Saul, was wishing more on his enemy than I could ever do. I think these opening five verses are a commentary on the rest of the Psalm:

'O God, whom I praise, do not remain silent, for wicked and deceitful men have opened their mouths against me; they have spoken against me with lying tongues. With words of hatred they surround me; they attack me without cause. In return for my friendship they accuse me, but I am a man of prayer. They repay me evil for good, and hatred for my friendship Appoint an evil man to oppose him; let an accuser stand at his right hand. When he is tried, let him be found guilty, and may his prayers condemn him.'

The following morning the phone rang at precisely 9 am. It was Norman Warren. This was the first opportunity I had to report on the Pastoral Committee Meeting. Norman listened with interest, and not a little surprise at how the proceedings had gone. He said he had seen a draft copy of the minutes and, as a result, had been to see the Bishop.

'Over the weekend I wrote him a long letter,' he said, 'relating the history, the problems, and the progress. Posting the letter in Bishopscourt yesterday the Bishop opened the door and invited me in. I told him that I had been commissioned by the previous Bishop to see the scheme through and, on more than one occasion, it had received the approval of the Pastoral Committee. He gave me a good hearing and I warned him against voices that were permanently against progress in this area. I, like you, sincerely hope that the revised scheme, going to the Church Commissioners, will have his approval. I thought you'd be interested to know!'

It was March 21st. Celia and I, with Jamie, Lesley and Dick were going off to a Reform Conference at Swanwick. This coincided with the Diocesan Board of Finance meeting and our scheme was high on the agenda, and ready for a decision by the Board. We arrived at Church House at 1:45 pm. I spotted Ian Fawkner, the Chairman of the Board of Finance, and Dennis Barden, the Diocesan Treasurer. They were chatting outside. We made our way into the cathedral to spend time in prayer while the meeting continued. There were dozens of Hungarian students in there, so we chose a small side-chapel in order to avoid the constant throng of tourists. After a short time of prayer, I left the others and went to the church office. At 2:15 pm the Bishop opened with prayer. Following the minutes of the previous meeting, the chairman then began the current agenda: 'Item 20.'

Our proposals were announced. I took a quick glance at those members likely to oppose the new church scheme; they were sitting together.

Norman Warren was invited by the Chairman to present the Christ Church proposals. He stood up and made the point that the committee members had received all the financial facts and if there were any queries regarding this, he would answer accordingly. He then sat down. I was dumbstruck! Dick had prepared two sides of A4 paper in giving clear instructions for Norman to present each of the financial items that were before the members. I fully expected him to be on his feet for at least ten minutes. It was unbelievable that he was afraid of a presentation, so I took the view that he fully intended to keep the facts to a minimum, and not produce further evidence that could only be used as ammunition against us. Now the questions came fast and furious from the opposition:

'Chairman, shouldn't the incumbent leave the room?'

'Please could we be informed of the name of the party who is financing the shops to the tune of £100,000?'

'How much did the church raise annually?'

'What was the tithe the church gave annually to others?'

The answers to all these questions took some twenty minutes, and I found myself on my feet on at least five occasions. At precisely 2:40 pm the Chairman asked me to leave the room. I stepped outside and into the glorious sunshine of a cold spring day. In the tiny park opposite, the daffodils were still in full bloom. I was immediately encouraged by the positive statement that was emanating from God's lovely natural world.

Sitting on a wall nearby was Jamie. He said he had left the meeting in the Cathedral to see if there was anything to report back.

'Well they're now deliberating it Jamie. It sure is decision time!' I pronounced.

'I'll go and tell the others,' he suggested.

I walked back into reception and nervously approached the committee door. There was no sign of anyone heading in my direction to invite me back into the meeting. The automatic door opened behind me, and there was Robert Wickham.

'What's the position John?'

I related the events and told him that Jamie and Dick, Leslie and Celia were in the cathedral side chapel praying for God's direction and decision.

We walked upstairs and immediately met Brenda Hurd.

'It's decision time for us Brenda!'

'John,' she responded, 'you're a man of great faith, you have come this far and God will not let you down now, so keep trusting.'

Outside again we were all nervously pacing up and down the pavement when behind me I heard a voice.

'John!'

I spun around. A tall gentleman had opened the door to the committee room and beckoned to me. His face was bright and he was smiling. Was he trying to tell me something? All eyes rested upon me as I made my way across the room to the far side and sat down. I shot a glance to my right and John Kirby (a friend from Tunbridge Wells, whom I had known for a number of years) stuck out his left thumb, pointing to the ceiling. I knew, at that moment that we had got our approval. The Chairman spoke.

'After some deliberation, John, the committee's voting was as follows: twenty-six votes in favour, one against, and seven abstentions. The Christ Church scheme will now go to the Church Commissioners after the Bishop has given his approval.'

'Chairman,' I said, 'may I take this opportunity of thanking the members for supporting the building of the new church in Tunbridge Wells. I am truly a very happy man today! Would you be so kind as to accept my apology for leaving the meeting now as I have a conference to attend at Swanwick in Derbyshire.' I picked up my papers and briefcase and walked out of the committee room.

Robert and Dick were waiting outside. With bended arm and clenched fist I shouted softly, 'We've got it!'

Dick seemed to wilt physically as all the tension of the moment drained from him. Robert gave a large sigh of relief.

'Let's hope it's easier with the Commissioners!' he said.

As we strolled back into the Cathedral, I began to relax and unwind, and felt a lump in my throat and liquid in the back of my eyes. We said nothing as we moved into the side chapel. Lesley and Celia were bent over in prayer. Jamie was missing. The girls didn't hear us approach, and I just said, 'Praise God — We've got permission!'

Celia leapt to her feet, threw her arms around my neck and cried with the utmost relief, 'Praise God darling... Oh! praise God.'

There were hugs and tears all round, in the middle of which Jamie returned.

'What's happened?' he whispered in a half panic, seeing us in tears.

'We've got permission,' I replied.

'Thank God for that!' he whispered. 'I thought for a moment it had failed!'

Back outside the Cathedral, with the remnants of Rochester Castle looking down upon us, I duly thanked everyone, and four of us set off for the Conference. The relief from the burden of the day was near ecstatic, and now we were in the right frame of mind to enjoy the next few days together.

Chapter 16

Round and round the mulberry bush

On Friday 12th May, I received a letter from Martin Ellengorn, one of the senior civil servants at Millbank, in which he stated that the Bishop of Rochester had officially withdrawn the previous scheme under Section 15 of the Pastoral Measure. This tied a pink bow around all the paperwork of the previous twelve years and consigned it to the bowels of Church House. Another section would surely have placed all the paperwork on hold, and as all the issues were about the demolition of the old building, and almost little or nothing had been written about the new scheme, it was therefore imperative that we meet with the officers and with the Archdeacon of Rochester, who was the Diocesan Board of Finances representative on our Building Committee.

1 Millbank in Westminster is directly across the road from the Houses of Parliament. It is a large imposing structure with marble halls and a wide impressive stone staircase. An old-fashioned central lift dominated the main foyer. Jamie, Dick, John and I were met by an official who took us to the conference room. This was a large room with an oak panelled high ceiling with an oval table in the centre. Already seated was Robert Banfield (with whom I had spoken many times on the telephone), Alan Guthrie-Jones (who was always most helpful and sympathetic to our church building scheme), and Martin Ellengorn, who was seated in the principal chair. We were joined by the Archdeacon, the Church Commissioner's Legal Representative, and a young lady taking notes.

Mr. Ellengorn outlined a potted history as to how we had reached the present position. He was quite clear that the Bishop's reference to Section 15 was an act which would totally withdraw the previous scheme, and thus end this chapter in the life of the proposed new building.

'A new project has now been proposed,' he said with some authority, 'And therefore it must be treated by the Commissioners as a totally new programme in its own right.'

Despite various protestations, and after forty-five minutes of debate, the civil servants of the church could only move within the letter of the law as stated by the previous Bishop, quoting the appropriate Act.

'I don't think you should be too disheartened Reverend Banner,' began Guthrie-Jones, 'As I see it, you could have the Royal Assent by February of next year, but you must understand that there are certain statutory procedures which we must adhere to, and certain delays — again established in law — for genuine objectors to the scheme. We are very sympathetic and will do all in our power to execute this scheme as quickly as possible.'

The Archdeacon concurred, and after shaking hands, we left the building.

Some seven weeks later, on July 11th, Dick Warren and I were again journeying up to London. This time we were heading to the Lands Tribunal in Chancery Lane. This summer was about to break all previous records. Having had a comparatively dry Spring, Britain was now experiencing temperatures in the nineties, with high humidity levels. To put it bluntly, every day was a sticky day, and this day was no exception. On the journey Dick and I reflected on a meeting earlier in the year in which the principal players had met around the long conference table at Gleeds' office in Tunbridge Wells. Present were; The Four Just Men, Ross Savage (a partner with the firm) and his assistant Paul Sweeney. Also present were David Grayston (architect) and his assistant Simon Glenister. Dick had produced the figures and had projected the cost of the scheme over its building period, including interest that would accrue. From this arithmetical exercise we were £160,000 short of the lowest Tender price from BMP. Some moments dripped by, and furtive glances were shared around the table. I broke the silence with the words: 'God will supply all our needs, and of that I have no doubt!'

'The point is John, that we must prove that we have the money otherwise we would be accused of fraudulent mismanagement. Therefore a list of savings must be made,' interrupted John Kain.

'I agree with you John,' said Dick.

Paul Sweeney agreed to make the list with the help of others. Within a week I had the list on my desk and it looked pretty devastating. The character of floor, ceilings, and overall decor would be adversely affected.

The compulsory purchase order (CPO) had thus far given us a compensation figure of £500,000 plus interest back-dated to when the order came into effect. The Tunbridge Wells District Valuation Officer had seen fit to award a further £100,000. Robert Wickham felt we were nearing a position of settlement. I, for my part, wanted to hold out for £750,000, but I was prepared to acknowledge that this extra £100,000 offered was a compromise step, which we would have to meet, hence the desire to get £650,000.

The previous evening the Parochial Church Council had, on the advice of Robert Wickham, passed a resolution that acceptance of the sealed offer of £600,000 should be agreed if we could do no better. With this further £100,000 and the interest that would accrue, we were not far short of the £160,000 needed to put back our savings.

Dick and I boarded our train for the city, keeping our conversation low in case members of the Borough Council were within ear-shot. A short taxi ride and we were in Chancery Lane and at the Lands Tribunal building. Robert was already waiting for us, surrounded by an assortment of files and boxes and a suitcase containing all the evidence he had amassed over a period of seven or eight years. He introduced us to Martin, the surveyor who was to give evidence if required, of various valuations and costings.

Robert was pacing up and down the open public area, which was now vacant, with his mobile phone. Within a matter of minutes our Advocate Solicitor arrived. Peter Scrafton's professionalism was evident by the relaxed mood, his understanding of our case, and the determined line that he was going to take upon our behalf. I warmed to him immediately.

It was now shortly after 10 am and Peter began explaining how things would develop. The 'judge' in the Tribunal is actually referred to as 'The Member.' In fact, he is a Chartered Surveyor and would be hard at work in his office upstairs. Shortly, Peter would advise the member's clerk that the parties are still engaged in pre-hearing negotiations and please would he delay coming down until he is requested. It was hoped that an 'out-of-court' settlement would satisfy both parties. Peter explained that, once the Member enters the court room, a fee of £3,000 is triggered! The Member sent down a message that if it came to a hearing, then gentlemen would be allowed to remove their jackets! We carried on in our windowless conference room, sweltering in spite of the air conditioning. At 10:25 am Peter suggested that it was time we had a coffee, and explained this could be obtained from a little cafe down the road. He pulled me to one side and whispered with a little glint in his eye.

'You see, this is what happens. In a little while I walk down the road, get my little paper bag from the tea kiosk and, complete with bun, I make my way back to the court. The solicitor acting for the other clients usually meets me half-way down the street, and we discuss the case and our part in it, with a view to moving towards a settlement,' he explained with assurance.

Neil, acting for Tunbridge Wells Borough Council, had faxed Peter a transcript of their submission at half-past-eleven the previous night, and Peter had been studying this in the train on the way to the hearing. At one point he disappeared and for over half-an-hour spoke to Neil regarding a settlement. It would appear that the other side were not going to budge from £600,000 and therefore Peter assured them that we would 'see them in court!'

Dick and I went for a coffee. Upon our return we were met by Peter in the entrance hall. The other side were prepared to negotiate he informed us. They were shifting from their intransigent position and looking at Robert's figures afresh! Dick and I felt like two redundant fairies at a pantomime, watching but not taking part. Peter approached us and said, 'Now's the time to start praying!' So we did, in full view of the desk clerk, who appeared to treat us as onlookers to the drama.

After much to-ing and fro-ing the solicitors returned to their clients. A final figure was reached which brought an end to the dispute. It was agreed that we settle at £620,000, plus accrued interest, and the Borough Council paying all the solicitors and surveyors fees, which, at a guess, could have been in excess of

£50,000! The relief on Robert's face was a picture of victory, triumph and peace. We collected our bags, put on our jackets and called a taxi. We piled in the back. I shot a glance at Peter and began to sing: 'If I were a rich man, yubba-dubba…'

Immediately he joined in, and the rest started laughing. A clap of thunder disturbed the joviality of the occasion. Leaving our bags at Robert's office we proceeded to a celebration lunch together.

After the meal Dick and I went to the Church Commissioners Office and gave a verbal report to Alan Guthrie-Jones. He was delighted and explained to us that there was still three weeks to the deadline for objectors to the scheme to write in, but so far none had been received, though he had received forty-six letters supporting the scheme. Dick and I journeyed back in the train and reflected on the fact that we had made £160,000 worth of savings, and now, with a settlement of a further £120,000, plus the interest over a number of years, God had met all our needs, and these savings would not have to be made. Within weeks we had a total of four letters from individuals against the scheme, including one from the Rural Dean and one from the Deanery Lay Chairman.

The Sunday following the Tribunal, I was able to tell the congregation the good news. That gave us all a time of rejoicing and encouragement. It was yet another sign of his promise: *'I will supply all your needs according to my riches in glory'*. This was truly a vindication of my earlier activity at a PCC meeting when faint hearts were not prepared to see that we could go ahead with the cost of the building faced with such a shortfall.

A two week holiday was now due and Miles, who had now gained his driving licence, took us to Gatwick airport and we flew out to Mahon on the Island of Minorca, one of the Balearic Islands. Nicola, now twenty-three, was working for Thomson's, and after clearing the baggage claim in the airport concourse, we saw her in her red and blue uniform, complete with smiling face. She was thrilled to see, Celia, Kerry and myself, and after big hugs all round she spoke a little Spanish to the driver of the coach and we were on our way to Cala Galdana, on the west coast of the island. Life with Nickles was something to be experienced. Her happy-go-lucky, ebullient character was infectious. The party would not officially start until she arrived, and that's when the laughter and the jokes and the music seemed to commence. One memorable evening we took a coach, laden with tourists, to Casa Blanca, some forty minutes drive near the old capital of Ciudedela. The Thomson's representatives were enterainers for the evening at Pedro's Bar. Pedro himself was a larger than life figure, armed with a Spanish guitar, who in the course of the evening entertained us along with the Thomson's representatives. We all enjoyed a three course meal. Nicola, with the others, danced on the stage and then at one point, later in the evening, the curtains opened to reveal her standing there with a microphone in her hand. The music began, and our eldest daughter sang "Stand by your man" to the delight of everyone present. She received applause, and Celia and I, glancing at one another, were very proud.

Within a matter of days, Nickles and José (a friend from the hotel) with the three of us were in Mahon searching the town for a wedding outfit for Nickles. Our second son Christopher was marrying Claire on 30th September, and Thomson's would not release Nickles until the 29th, so it was imperative to buy an outfit quickly. As we gazed in the various shops it was soon quite clear that my tastes would have ideally suited a women of 72 years of age!

'Oh Dad, get with it. You're old-fashioned!'

'I wouldn't be seen dead in that!'

'Ideal for a funeral! Okay for Cruft's Dog Show! Get with it Dad!'

Celia whispered, 'Darling will you be quiet. They know what they are looking for!'

That was me put in my place so José and I practised our Spanish and English. I particularly wanted to learn Spanish for I was hoping to go out to Guatemala to see the work of the Toybox Charity, which had been started by two young members of our congregation, Duncan and Jenni Dyason. Meanwhile, the ladies were still fussing over clothes, and after a couple of hours, and me £182 lighter in pocket, the outfit was purchased and we made out way back to Santa Tomas. The following morning José took us to the airport.

Within a matters of days I received a call from Robert Banfield, one of the Church Commissioners' civil servants. He informed me that our papers had left the diocese, that is, they had gone through all the various committees and received the Bishop's signature, and were now to be discussed on September 13th. He would be in touch regarding the result a day or two later. As always, I informed the congregation in good time, and there followed much prayer for the right decision

The 13th came and went. The 14th came and went. No news from the Commissioners. On the morning of the 15th, I rang their offices in London.

'I'm interested to know what the final outcome was of the meeting two days ago.'

Alan Guthrie-Jones replied, 'Well John, no one is in opposition to the scheme, but certain points need to be clarified, so a letter has gone to Rochester Church House. We shall have a meeting to discuss the same before the end of the month with representatives from the diocese, and I have every reason to believe that the matter will go forward for approval.'

The conversation over, I reflected on the endless round of committees and immediately a horrible grey coldness swept over me, like a cold icy fog, blurring, confusing, wet, dank, depressing and grey… grey… grey.

Within the hour Robert Wickham rang me.

'John, I've got to see the Bishop regarding this next meeting. Unfortunately I'm on an enquiry in the Midlands and won't be able to make it.'

Within forty-eight hours, Robert had spoken to Celia and informed her that his meeting with the Bishop had gone superbly well, and that the Bishop was most supportive of our scheme. However, he had gone down with the flu and would not be attending the meeting. I had fears of the repetition of previous meetings, where supporters of the scheme could not attend, leaving the decision making to those who opposed the scheme. In other words, my voting power was disintegrating! Again, within a few days, I was informed by David Gater, that Peter Law (a long time supporter of the scheme) would be on holiday and so David would be representing Peter. There was no question that David was a good man, but he had no deep insight into the long term agony that I and the congregation had suffered, but he was a very positive supporter nonetheless. Without asking him concerning the clarification, I knew only too well that the objectors were raising issues such as the financial viability and the lack of ecumenical consultation, and added to this the general point — did the Church of England require to re-build in Tunbridge Wells when there were so many other churches?

Guthrie-Jones informed me that one of the senior civil servants of the Commissioners, Martin Ellengorn, would be present at the meeting. So I informed David Gater that I would write to the Commissioners giving them some background material. I sent a copy of these papers to the Archdeacon of Rochester and reassured him that we would be praying as the meeting got under way, and requested that he ring me the moment the meeting was over.

The following week, on the day of the meeting, I telephoned a number of people including, Erica Holland, Lesley Still (whom I asked to inform others), Carol Wharton, Flo Billson (who was approaching 103 years young, with a mind as alert as a cricket) and Audrey Danby (an ex-missionary from Uganda), and Pym (who prayed with her daily help, Janice). Thus armed with this solid phalanx of prayer I eagerly awaited the result of the meeting. The Phone rang.

'John, Norman here. Just thought I'd report on the meeting this morning. All the objections were met head on and... thank you for your paperwork in backing up our argument. The Bishop could not attend the meeting but he had earlier sent a letter to the Commissioners giving no less than eleven points in favour of the new church! Paul Williams, the Bishop's chaplain, was superb, and I believe the Church Commissioners, under the Chairmanship of Lady Laird, returned to London totally satisfied that the scheme would now go through the Privy Council and receive the Royal Assent by the end of the year!'

'Norman, thank you most sincerely for all your hard work — I would like to think that this is the end of circling the mulberry bush, but we still have to receive the approval of the full board of the Church Commissioners Pastoral Committee, and I am hoping that Robert Banfield will let me know the result. Well done! Let's keep in touch,' I replied.

Chapter 17

The edge of an adventure

On the morning of October 12th I journeyed to Rochester to attend the Pastoral Committee. Within a matter of minutes the Bishop's Chaplain sat at my left, later to be joined by Chris Collins, now at Christ Church in Luton. We passed the time making small talk, chatting about family and friends. He asked about Christopher and Claire's wedding. Chris Collins had been with me from the beginning, from meeting me off the train on my first sight of Tunbridge Wells, through all the traumas of trying to get the new church built, and now, here we were eagerly awaiting the result of the Church Commissioners Pastoral Committee Meeting, which had met some ten days earlier.

'I haven't heard from the Church Commissioners yet,' I whispered to him. Two days after the meeting I had phoned Robert Banfield, and was promptly told that it was inappropriate to know the decision until the Bishop had been informed. At that moment a hand touched my arm, and Paul whispered to me, 'You have *full* approval!'

'I haven't heard officially!' I whispered.

'Well, it's true. You now have the authority of the Commissioners!'

'Well…!' I said with some glee in my voice, 'Anyone brought a bottle of champagne to the meeting?'

By now there were half of the assembled members seated and the Bishop, as Chairman, shot a glance at both of us.

'Is there something to celebrate?' he asked.

We did not respond. The meeting commenced.

Within the space of some twenty-five minutes an item on the Agenda read, 'Holy Trinity with Christ Church, Tunbridge Wells. Rebuilding Scheme.'

'And now to the Tunbridge Wells item. Is, uh, there anything to report?' the Bishop asked as he shot a glance to Peter Law, the Diocesan Secretary.

'No, sir,' Peter replied graciously.

'David?'

David Gater looked down at his papers and also replied, 'No, sir.'

'Then we await the decision, and move on to our next item.'

'Well,' I thought, 'How is it that the Bishop's Chaplain can tell me it's through, and yet the Bishop has not reported the matter?'

My thoughts went back to Robert Banfield's remark, that no one could be informed until the Bishop had received official confirmation. If the Bishop has received the news, why did he not announce it? And then, I realised that an objector to the scheme was in fact present at the meeting and quite likely had not been officially informed in writing. Now I knew why David Gater had told me over the phone that morning: 'The decision of the Commissioners is imminent.' But not to be told left me pondering.

'Apologies!' the Bishop's Chaplain whispered in my left ear. My immediate reaction by now was fairly predictable. My emotions were being played about with yet again. First I'm down, then I'm up, and then I'm down again.

The Bishop closed the meeting with a prayer, I remained seated quietly collecting my papers together, when a sudden tap on my left shoulder disturbed my thoughts. It was Norman Warren.

'John, can I have a quick word?'

He beckoned me with his right finger into the corner of the room.

'I couldn't tell you earlier, but the Church Commissioners have given the scheme their full approval, and the matter will now go up to the Privy Council, and then on to the Royal Assent.'

Norman's voice was filled with reassurance, and not a little excitement. In the latter stages of the scheme he had travelled with me through the hurts and frustrations, and now here we were together quietly rejoicing about the result. We were interrupted by Paul who whispered to me in the hearing of Norman, 'That was my first mistake!'

Paul quite clearly knew the result and should have been obliged to keep it to himself.

Journeying home I was excited about who should know the good news. Naturally Celia would be the first to know, but having suffered so much heartaches and tears, and having prayed for so long, I could predict that her reaction would be a quiet acquiescence to the plan and purpose of God. It would be no shriek of excitement of a child, no Christmas morning elation, but just the strong belief in faith and prayer, and in the confidence of our relationship with God; that this was the expected result from which we had not ceased to waiver. So it was over the table at tea that we shared this quiet joy and the confirmation that we were in the centre of God's will and doing his purpose.

I rang John Kain at home and his response was very much that of Christmas morning. A moderate exclamation, a bit onomatopoeic and a break in the voice with the words, 'I could almost cry! Praise the Lord!'

The approval from the Church Commissioners had passed through its main Pastoral Committee on 10th October. This was our wedding anniversary: 'What a nice present from God,' I thought. A delay of one month, which was laid down by statute, would mean that by November 10th that period would be complete, and the scheme would be in the hands of the Privy Council to receive approval on November 14th. Robert Banfield rang me from the Church Commissioners to inform me that of the four objectors, three had dropped out. We were quite content that the mind of the diocese was now approving the scheme, but one man, an ordinary member of the public from Tunbridge Wells, was continuing to object and that they had received his letter on October 20th and that was allowed to stand for 28 days. Instead of the matter going to the Privy Council directly, it would now have to go to the Judicial sub-Committee of that body, and the Royal Assent could be delayed by some twelve weeks.

I replaced the telephone and shot a glance at Lesley, working on the computer at the opposite desk.

'Lesley, the devil is going to fight us all the way and at every hurdle. We must continue to pray on and keep our battle powder dry.'

She replied, somewhat nonchalantly, 'What's new!'

'Wouldn't it be a wonderful Christmas present for my congregation receiving the Royal Assent a few days before Christmas?'

The word at Ilfracombe came back to me: 'Christmas'.

'Lesley, what do I tell the congregation? Do I have a right to protect them from this disappointment? '

'No,' she replied, 'We have been naked with the truth so far, so let's continue in that vein.'

With that we both rested easy and committed the matter to prayer.

On Sunday January 21st we had a congregational celebration for the marriage of Jamie Austin, the Churchwarden, to Veronica Whitley our Pastoral Assistant. Due to shortage of seats, I sat on the stage in one corner of the hall eating my meal. I looked at some eighty-five people, realising that many of them had been with me in the beginning as far back as 1982. Like the children of Israel we had been in a wilderness, not forty years, but fourteen years. Somehow time, and adversity, had given us a treasured pleasure and empathy with each other. We had prayed together, fasted together, shared together. It had been a time of sifting. Some had left when we moved out of the old church, others left because I refused to be shaken from my vision, which had become a 'vision of the congregation'. It is true that my leadership at times had been autocratic, though always bathed in love, but now here we were with £1.2 million pounds in the bank, waiting for the last hurdle to be overcome. I loved them all, including the ones who had given me pain. Now here we were celebrating together and I silently prayed, 'Lord, perhaps in the near future we will celebrate and praise you together when the Royal Assent is given for our new church.'

The following morning Lesley came in at 9 o'clock with her usual soprano warble, 'Morning!' By 9:20 am I joined her in the office. Our first job was to read the mail, followed by morning prayer together. I took one of the *Morning By Morning* books. On this occasion I used the one by Spurgeon. I read the text: *'Son of man, What is the vine tree more than any tree or than a branch which is amongst the trees of the forest?'* (Ezekiel 15:2). The comment on the text continued:

These words are for the humbling of God's people; but they are called God's vine, but what are they by nature more than others? They by God's goodness, have become fruitful, having been planted in a good soil; the Lord hath trained them upon the walls of the sanctuary, and they bring forth fruit to his glory; but what are they without their God? What are they without the continual influence of the spirit, begetting fruitfulness in them?

Commenting on the passage together I was assured in the knowledge that any fruitfulness borne by us was all of God's grace and God's spirit.

At 3:15 pm Lesley answered the telephone, put her finger over the 'mute' button and announced that it was the Church Commissioners. A pleasant voice announced, 'Church Commissioners here, Mr. Banner. I have some very good news for you! The Law Lords have refused the objector's leave to appeal to the Privy Council, and therefore at its next meeting, it will recommend to Her Majesty that the Royal Assent be granted to you to demolish and re-build on your present site!'

'Thank you very much. That's good news!' I slowly and methodically replaced the receiver.

I sat gazing at Lesley across the desk. Some fifteen to twenty seconds drifted by and I was steeling myself to announce the news.

'We have permission to go ahead with the scheme!' I told her softly, almost unknowingly.

'Thank God — That's brilliant news.'

Neither of us spoke for well over a minute and a half. I can best describe my feelings at this point as if one had just accomplished a very long journey in which one had encountered the frozen heights of the mountains, the heat and swamps of the valleys, the pain of climbing and trudging, and all the time carrying a seventy-pound burden. Doesn't the Scripture say, *'My strength is made perfect in your weakness'?* Bruised and broken, nevertheless I had an inner peace that the long trek was now over.

Lesley got up from her desk and came round to me. She gave me a large hug and whispered, 'Well done good and faithful servant!'

I replied, 'As a congregation we've been through a lot. My only fear now is that with the wilderness experience coming to an end, will we lose a lot of what we gained in adversity?'

A glance at my watch to look at the date, and from the time Banfield had rung me, it was exactly twelve weeks and two days since the last objecting letter was lodged!

I rang Celia at Burrswood and told her the news. She screamed, 'Hallelujah! Praise the Lord!' at the top of her voice, which clearly must have been heard by three or four other members of the staff.

'That's wonderful news Darling! Now let's get on and build!'

I put the phone down and wanted to cry. The feeling of release was more than I could bear. I wanted the freedom to shout my thanks to heaven. The middle of the garden would have been a good place to do it, but I decided to ring the rest of my friends and colleagues who had a just right to hear of the decision. And so I rang John Kain, who on hearing shouted: 'Yippee — Do you want a big kiss!'

I rang David Grayston, the architect: 'Congratulations John! Well done!'

I then rang Dick Warren and Joyce answered the telephone. In more sober tones, but with delight she said, 'Oh! John, that's wonderful news. I'll tell Dick the moment he comes in.'

I then asked Lesley to ring round people in the congregation and let them all know. From hereon, it was now downhill after the long hard struggle to reach the pinnacle of this moment.

Early that evening, around 5 pm, Carol Wharton rang to offer her congratulations and invited Celia and I to join her and John for a glass of champagne to celebrate her husband's birthday, to combine this with an extra glass to celebrate the go-ahead for the new church. This was a fitting end to the day.

The following day, Celia came in from her usual parish commitment of organising and running the 'Squeals on Wheels'. As she entered the door I shouted, 'I've put the soup on… I know it's early, but I have to be at a Diocesan Board of Finance Meeting this afternoon.'

At 1.50 pm I got in the car for a time of praise with the Lord over the decision from the Privy Council. I wondered what sort of reaction I would get upon entering Church House. I walked into the Conference room, and immediately bumped into Brenda Hurd.

'John, I'm so very, very thrilled at the good news. You must be over the moon!'

I gave her a hug, and my mind immediately went back to the time when the previous scheme had been thrown out by this Board, and dejected and down cast, I had gone up to her office and shared my innermost disappointments and anger, almost to the point of tears.

She had listened intently and with a lot of sympathy. With comforting words she had reassured me, 'Your day will come! If God gave you a vision and a calling, he will accomplish it.'

Today all that was fulfilled, and I was as much pleased for her as I was for myself.

My eye caught David Gater. He had sent a fax congratulating me and the PCC on gaining the permission from the Privy Council Law Lords. With a manly shake of the hand I assured him I was absolutely thrilled that we could now get started.

As a Board consisting of some thirty members we started this fresh session of 1996 with communion, followed by the meeting. Ian Fawkner, the Chairman, approached me with his hand outstretched and said, 'Happy New Year, John — we are all so thrilled at the news! Can I ask you to say a few words, under 'Matters Arising'?'

I concurred and made my way to the Minutes Secretary to the Board, Penny Law. Her face was a picture of joy as she said, 'Well done John, it's been a long time but you've made it!'

I thanked her and asked her if she would give me the exact verbiage that had come from the Privy Council. Armed with this I returned to my place and opened the agenda.

The meeting formally commenced and, within a matter of ten minutes, the Chairman invited me to say a few words regarding the latest news from the Privy Council. I stood up, and began.

'Ladies and Gentleman, I feel a kindred spirit with the Old Testament character, Jacob. On approaching his employer, who had two daughters, one prettier than the other, he enquired as to whether he might have the hand of the pretty one, Rachel. Laban, the father of the daughters, agreed on condition that Jacob serve as his Head Farmhand for seven years. At the end of that period Jacob was given the not-so-pretty daughter, and was politely informed by his new father-in-law, that he would have to work another seven years for the hand of Rachel. However, a week after he had married Leah, his father-in-law gave the hand of Rachel to Jacob, on the understanding that he would serve him for another seven years. He continued to serve Laban; thus fulfiling his contract. Fourteen years in all. Well, I feel a kindred spirit, and by the time our new building is erected, it will be fourteen years. I can tell you today that the Law Lords of the Privy Council will inform the Full Council in February that they are refusing the objectors further leave to appeal against the Christ Church Scheme.'

With that, I sat down. Behind me was one of the men who had so militantly opposed the scheme, and next to him a man that had worked so hard to see the scheme reach this point. They were chatting together, 'Well,' I thought, 'This is the Church of England... Some fearful to go forward... These people are non-visionary, non-prophetic, lacking faith and confidence, and working only with what we had and what we are — not placing confidence in God, but in men. There are others, bold, fearless, prepared to walk on water and live on the edge of an adventure. To attempt the impossible against all odds, and with the ability to carry people with them.'

The agenda dragged on and, as usual, began to hit it's all time low with a discussion on increasing each churches contribution to the Diocese, and thereby adding burdens to the majority of churches that were financially struggling. A certain element of doom and gloom fell over the meeting, and I increasingly became angry and frustrated. As children we had sung, 'He owns the cattle on a thousand hills, The wealth in every mine, He owns the rivers and the rocks and rills, The sun and stars that shine...' It was one thing to sing it in the comfort and naïvety of a well-lit Sunday School, and another to believe it in the cold sober confines of a meeting where men are only concerned with keeping the vision to within financial limits.

I left Church House with Norman Warren, and after a few pleasantries and comments on the scheme, I journeyed back to Tunbridge Wells intent upon examining my feelings about the events in the last forty-eight hours. On previous occasions, I had anticipated my reaction to be one of such elation that people would gather, champagne corks would pop, and there would be much slapping of backs and plenty of hale and hearty well-dones. Well, it didn't turn out like that at all. I had reached a stage some two years earlier when the only answer was to give God the whole responsibility for bringing this church into being. I would step out of the centre of the arena, find a convenient seat in the auditorium, and watch the events in a detached mood. What would be — would be!

Success, or failure, of the scheme was no longer my concern. If God doesn't care, then why should I? Yes, people had shaken my hand, slapped me on the back and said, 'Well done,' but how do you say these things to a spectator? The vision was God's. The faith I received, to fulfil the vision, was a gift from God. In all our disappointments and joys, God was at the centre of things, and he would not give his glory to anyone else. All the money raised, £1.25 million was his doing. And so my reaction was one of quiet reserve. What God had done — God had done! — and congratulations were due only to the Almighty.

On February 14th 1996, at the Court at Buckingham Palace, Her Majesty the Queen gave her Royal Assent for the demolition and rebuilding of Holy Trinity with Christ Church, Royal Tunbridge Wells.

The winning jockey in the Grand National Steeplechase is only as good as the horse upon which he rides. We had surmounted the final hurdle, having gone round the Aintree course twice, and coming over Beeches Brook was like jumping off the side of a mountain. We had our moments of fear, of deep disappointment, of prayer and fasting, of discord among ourselves, and times of great unity of purpose. In the end all was of God, for the benefit of his children, and the evangelistic outreach which would subsequently come to this parish of Royal Tunbridge Wells, and by missionary enterprise to that part of God's world well beyond the borders of the town.

> '*When the builders laid the foundation of the temple of the Lord, the priests in their vestments and with trumpets, and the Levites with cymbals, took their places to praise the Lord, as prescribed by David, King of Israel. With praise and thanksgiving they sang to the Lord; he is good; his love to Israel endures for ever. And all the people gave a great shout of praise to the Lord, because the foundation of the house of the Lord was laid.*'

Postscript

On September 19th 1997 the new Holy Trinity with Christ Church building was dedicated by the Bishop, The Rt. Rev. Dr. Michael Nazir-Ali, and the Christ Church Centre officially opened by Sir Patrick Mayhew, Member of Parliament for Royal Tunbridge Wells.

The building of the church was not without its difficulties. The contract was awarded to BMP plc and the work begun in May 1996. However, within twelve months, on April 1st to be precise, the vicar observed the builders leaving the site and the gates closed and locked. On asking the Site Manager, Adrian Talbot, "Was this a practical joke?", he simply replied, "My company have declared bankruptcy and are today going into receivership." However, within six weeks the contract was taken up by John Mowlem plc, and the work completed in time for the opening.

Today there stands in the heart of this Kent royal borough a well-designed and beautiful building to the praise and glory of God. With a well-managed coffee shop and open spacious narthex area, it has a warm and welcoming ambience. The worship area, with a seating capacity of 350, has already been filled on numerous occasions. The spacious parish hall is now used extensively for the community and the building has truly become a focal point at the southern end of the town.